'One of the greatest needs for preachers around the world
Wood's practical book keeps us focused on the Bible passa,
preaching that passage, and provokes warm relevance in o
has worked in many parts of the world with preachers who have greatly appreciated the clarity of the
'Action Steps' he has taught, and I am pleased to commend this title to a wider audience.'

Rev. Jonathan Lamb,
CEO and minister-at-large, Keswick Ministries,
former Director of Langham Preaching, Oxford, England

"As someone who has taught preaching for a dozen years, and served as a pastor for the 25 years before
that, and like Rodney, have facilitated preaching seminars in other cultures under the auspices of Langham
Preaching, I have come to realize that those of us who teach preaching have different ways of tackling the
task. But what almost all teachers of preaching – including equippers of Majority World preachers – find
challenging is coming up with a few clear principles and practices and then offering examples that flesh
them out. Rodney has done that in these pages; he has given us precept and example. The trainers that he
equips will no doubt devour this material and then digest it, make it their own contextualizing it in ways
that help their learners. Their sermons will look and sound different than mine and Rodney's – if we have
done our job well – but they will manifest the same respect for Scripture you will see in these pages. And
the Lord will be honored as his people hear his voice in the preached word and by it are strengthened to
do his will."

Greg R. Scharf, D. Min.
Professor of Pastoral Theology, Trinity Evangelical Divinity
School, Deerfield, IL, author of *Prepared to Preach, Relational
Preaching,* and, with John Stott, of *The Challenge of Preaching*

"Rev. Dr. Rodney Wood is a personal friend and a dear colleague of mine. One of the things we have in
common is an adamant commitment to 'expository preaching'. Dr. Wood's passion and zeal for this
subject are undeniable. His ability to teach and to tutor others on the knowledge and practice of expository
preaching has led him to produce this invaluable 'handbook' on the topic. This material is undoubtedly
a great tool in the formation of many other expository preachers, especially among those who do not
have the opportunities to access this kind of sound biblical and theological literature on the subject of
preaching. May the Lord of the Word bless Dr. Wood's effort of training others in the expository preaching
of His Word across the street and around the world."

Elias Medeiros, D.Min., D.Miss., Ph.D.
Harriet Barbour Professor of Missions
Reformed Theological Seminary, USA

"Rodney Wood has provided a very useful guide for pastors who want to interpret and preach the Bible
responsibly. The processes he recommends are balanced, wise and practical. Your ministry will be blessed
by this book."

Richard Pratt, Ph.D.
President, Third Millennium Ministries
Adjunct Professor of Old Testament
Reformed Theological Seminary, USA

"The preacher must be *faithful* to Scripture and clear to those who hear him. *Action Steps for Expository Preachers* addresses both of those areas in a thorough yet concise manner. Most resources like this simply address 'sermon preparation'. Rodney Wood has done the church a great service by taking it a step further and providing a practical, valuable, and reliable guide *for those who teach others,* so that the Word may be heard clearly to the ends of the earth. I have never seen material for training in sermon preparation in such a transferable and reproducible form. Thanks be to God!"

> T. Preston Pearce, Ph.D.
> Theological Education Consultant, Europe
> International Mission Board, Southern Baptist Convention

"Rodney Wood has given us a solid, practical handbook to teaching the basics of expository preaching. His practical experience and love for God's Word shine through every page. I heartily recommend this book for anyone who desires to improve his own preaching and especially those who, like me, want to be better teachers of expository preaching."

> Austin McCaskill, D. Min.
> Professor, Albanian Bible Institute (Durres)
> & Evangelical Theological Seminary (Sauk)

"*Action Steps for Expository Preachers* contains a gold mine of practical and biblical information for pastors and teachers. It will enable the pastor/teacher to rightly divide God's word and present it in a clear and understandable manner. It not only provides a resource to know how to study and preach the word, but it also gives spiritual insight for preparation and practical guidelines for interpreting and applying the message. I highly recommend this study for anyone wanting to learn how to effectively minister God's word to His people."

> Dr. Sammy Tippit
> International Evangelist, Conference Speaker, and Author

"The Gospel depends on Spirit guided communication and *Action Steps* opens effective biblical preaching to a worldwide audience by teaching the essential practices every preacher needs to know and develop."

> Dr. D. Greg Hauenstein
> President, MINTS, Miami International Seminary

"I thoroughly commend this book to any aspiring preacher or student of the Word. Having used it widely amongst pastors and evangelists in Tanzania we have found that it provides an excellent guide to engaging meaningfully with the text. If followed, the outcome is not just a sermon that is clear, relevant and faithful to the Biblical message, but also the spiritual transformation of the preacher and his congregation."

> Rev. Tony Swanson
> Coordinator of the Institute of Bible and Ministry
> African Inland Mission
> Morogoro, Tanzania

ACTION STEPS
FOR EXPOSITORY PREACHERS

A Method of Sermon Preparation

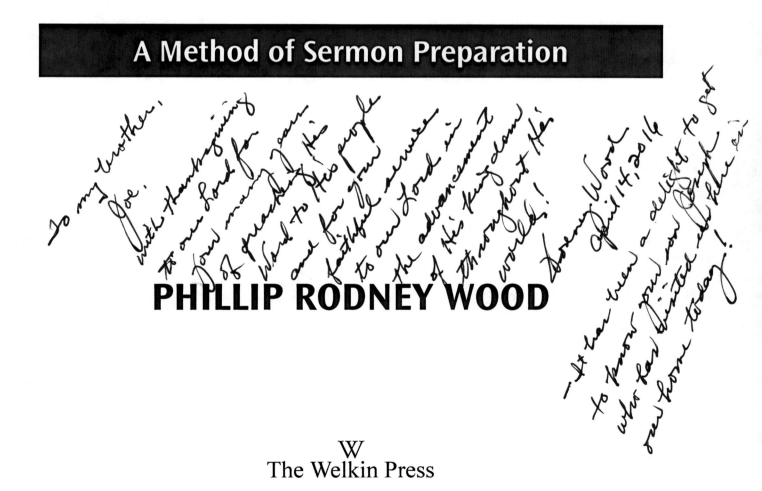

PHILLIP RODNEY WOOD

W
The Welkin Press

Action Steps for Expository Preachers, A Method of Sermon Preparation
Copyright © Phillip Rodney Wood 2011

ISBN: 978-0-9839217-0-7

Printed in the United States of America

Library of Congress Control Number: 2011917062

Cover Design by Larry Taylor of The Livingstone Corporation

The Welkin Press
1975 Myrtledale Ave.
Baton Rouge, LA 70808

To my wife, Becky,
my sons, Jake, Jim, and John,
and my daughter Rebecca Elizabeth, now with the Lord

TABLE OF CONTENTS

Acknowledgements

I would like to express my appreciation to the board of directors of The Mission Foundation for their personal supportiveness with regard to this project. Also, I am extremely grateful to those who read the manuscript and offered valuable comments and suggestions: Earl Adams, Richard Pratt, Walt Rogers, Greg Hauenstein, Ken Perez, Preston Pearce, Elias Medeiros, Austin McCaskill, Jonathan Lamb, Simon Vibert, Tony Swanson, Sammy Tippit, Gordon Woolard, and Greg Scharf.

I also want to thank my sons, Jake, Jim, and John, for their enthusiastic support of me in this work. And I of course want to thank my wife Becky with whom I have traveled and lived and served in many places in God's world. Countless times she has listened to me and prayed for me as I have preached and taught. She has counseled me and encouraged me like no one else. Thank you, Bec.

Finally, I will forever be grateful to my brother John Stott for the loving interest that he first took in me and my family when I was a young man studying at The London Institute for Contemporary Christianity. I am thankful for the friendship we enjoyed for twenty-seven years and for his many kindnesses to us. But I want to especially mention my gratitude to him for the privilege of being a part of the Langham Preaching team and for the personal words of encouragement he gave me concerning the experience I would have as a teacher in the ongoing development of my lectures for expository preaching seminars.

The Purpose of This Book

Equipping preachers to train other preachers in the skill of expository preaching: This is the purpose for which these lecture notes, worksheets, and examples have been assembled.

This is material that I have developed over the past several years while serving as a facilitator for Langham Preaching (John Stott Ministries) seminars in African and Central/Eastern European countries. While engaged in this work, I have profited greatly from interaction with my colleagues and our national hosts. I am very appreciative of those men (as well as some other friends) who have given me helpful critique of both my earlier and later efforts in writing and teaching on expository preaching.

However, I am especially indebted to my good friend Rev. Tony Swanson, who serves with African Inland Mission in Tanzania. While we were serving together in Mwanza in 2007, Tony encouraged me to develop "action steps" in my lectures. That week I began to formulate those action steps, and I have employed this approach since that time.

The sermon preparation process presented in this book includes two main parts: Studying the Bible Passage and Writing Your Sermon. The first of these has been divided into two lectures because of the amount of material involved, whereas the second part (Writing Your Sermon) is covered in one lecture.

The method given here is useful in handling many passages of the Bible. However, in dealing with certain genre (for example, narrative, poetry, proverbs, parables, and apocalyptic literature), you will find that although certain principles in this book will be helpful, you will not be able to apply all of the methodology to all genres in the same way. Also, this book will not include lecture material on matters that pertain specifically to the various types of biblical literature.

Along with the lecture notes, there are worksheets and a list of suggested passages for workshops in which a handful of delegates/students study a Bible passage together and develop theme statements and outlines for a sermon. There are also two appendices: Appendix 1 includes examples of sermon theme statements and outlines, and Appendix 2 provides an example of our entire process of going from the biblical text to the sermon manuscript.

In addition to our "action step" lectures, I have decided to include two additional lectures. The first of these is on hermeneutics (principles of interpretation) and the other is concerning the matter of application. I would like to suggest that you not give these additional lectures until after you have covered the first three lectures and have allowed your delegates/students to participate in a workshop in which they apply the "action steps" given in lectures 1-3.

My prayer is that these lecture notes and instruments will be helpful to preachers who want to go and train other preachers, whether in national or regional seminars or in small groups or one-to-one situations. I would like to emphasize that this material is for facilitators/trainers/teachers. This is not a syllabus for the students/delegates and therefore should not be given to them before the lectures are given. They should only receive the handouts and worksheets that are provided on pages 30-35. However, I hope that you will consider giving the delegates/students a copy of all the lecture notes and some extra worksheets (or, if possible, a copy of this book) at the end of the training program so that they can go and train others.

Rodney Wood

INSTRUCTIONS FOR TEACHERS/FACILITATORS
Regarding Worksheets and Outlines

Before you begin lecturing, please distribute copies of the following worksheets which are provided at the back of this book:

    1) Study the Context (p. 30)

    2) Write Notes on the Details of Each Verse (p. 31)

    3) Side <u>A</u> – The Outline and Main Idea of the Biblical Passage (p. 32)

    4) Side <u>B</u> – Theme Statement and Outline of Your Sermon (p. 33)

Also, distribute copies of the lecture outlines:

    Studying the Bible Passage (Side A) – This outline is for Part One, which includes the <u>first two lectures</u>: Studying the Context and Studying the Content. (p. 34)

    Writing Your Sermon (Side B) – This is the outline for Part 2, which is comprised only of the <u>third lecture</u>. (p. 35)

PART ONE
Studying The Bible Passage

LECTURE ONE
STUDYING THE CONTEXT
Three Action Steps

INTRODUCTORY COMMENTS

The Bible is the inerrant, infallible Word of God. In 2 Peter 1:20-21, the Apostle Peter says, "knowing this first of all, that no prophecy of Scripture comes from someone's own interpretation. For no prophecy was ever produced by the will of man, but men spoke from God as they were carried along by the Holy Spirit. Human writers were "carried along by the Holy Spirit" in such a way that every word they wrote was "from God." In his second letter to Timothy, the Apostle Paul writes, "All Scripture is breathed out by God and profitable for teaching, for reproof, for correction, and for training in righteousness." (2 Timothy 3:16). All of the words of the Bible are inspired by God.

Eternal God has spoken, and He is still speaking through Holy Scripture. We who are preachers and teachers have been granted the great privilege and the tremendous responsibility of explaining to others what Almighty God has said.

We are not to use the Bible as merely a source text from which we develop our own messages. The Bible is the message! We are to take God's message to the men, women, and children of this world.

We must remember that we are not entertainers. We are the explainers of God's Word!

In the performing of this great task, we should look to the example of Ezra. In Ezra 7:10, we read, "For Ezra had set his heart to study the law of the Lord, and to do it and to teach His statutes and rules in Israel."

Notice the order given in this verse. Ezra devoted himself first to study God's Word and then to "do" it before he would go on to teach it. So we as God's servants must also diligently study the Word and apply it to our own lives before we teach it. We should not be teaching what we are not seeking to apply to ourselves. And we cannot make proper application of truth that we do not understand. Like Ezra, we must study. We must give ourselves to the work of exegesis.

What is exegesis? "Exegesis is the careful, systematic study of Scripture to discover the original, intended meaning."[1] In exegesis we are studying to understand what the original author (or speaker – for example, Jesus in giving the Sermon on the Mount) was saying to the people to whom he was writing (or speaking) at that time.[2]

We must ask "What did this text mean to those people who lived long ago in another place?" – "What was the biblical author saying to those people who first received his writing?"[3]

---

1   Gordon Fee and Douglas Stuart, *How to Read the Bible for All Its Worth*, p. 19.
2   There are of course some instances in which the author is providing words of prophecy which he himself does not fully understand. Peter talks about this in 1 Peter 1:10-12.
3   Also, as Richard Pratt has said, "What should the original audience have understood?"

For example, we must ask:

- "What was Paul saying to the Romans?"
- "What was Moses saying to the people of Israel?"
- "What was Isaiah saying to the people of Judah?"

"A text means what its author meant."[4] John Stott warns that "to search for (the text's) contemporary message without first wrestling with its original meaning is to attempt a forbidden shortcut."[5] Dr. Stott gives us three reasons why we must not do this:

1. It dishonours God (disregarding his chosen way of revealing himself in particular historical and cultural contexts).
2. It misuses his Word (treating it like an almanac or a book of magic spells).
3. It misleads his people (confusing them about how to interpret Scripture).[6]

We must take no shortcuts. We must remember that it is the Word of Almighty God that we have been called to preach. We must handle it with great respect. We must work hard to know what God has said.

STUDYING THE CONTEXT
Going Back into the World of the Bible

We begin the study of our Bible passage by traveling back to the world of the author and the people to whom he was writing. As one scholar has said, the preacher "pulls up his chair to where the biblical authors sat."[7] As we sit there with the author and look around at his world, we must ask three questions: 1) What kind of literature is this? 2) What is the historical situation? and 3) What comes before and after this biblical passage that I am studying?

1. What kind of literature is this?

In the Bible, we find many different types of literature – letters, laws, parables, history, poetry, prophecy, proverbs, prayers, speeches, apocalyptic writing, and other forms. We must remember that each type of literature must be interpreted and applied in a certain way.

We will not address the issues involved in dealing with each kind of literature in this series of lectures. Those matters must be addressed in future lectures. For now we will only note that it is extremely important that we recognize the type of literature we are reading and that we seek to interpret it in a manner that is appropriate for that form of writing. We cannot properly interpret a Bible passage unless we first ask, "What kind of literature is this?"[8]

---

4   E. D. Hirsch, Validity in Interpretation, p. 1, quoted in John Stott's *Between Two Worlds*, p. 221. Also, see Walter C. Kaiser, Jr., *Toward An Exegetical Theology*, p. 31-36, for a discussion of Hirsch's views.
5   John Stott, *Between Two Worlds*, p. 221.
6   Ibid, p. 221.
7   Haddon Robinson, *Biblical Preaching*, p. 23.
8   Several helpful sources on biblical genre: Gordon Fee and Douglas Stuart, *How to Read the Bible for All Its Worth*, p. 45-245; Graeme Goldsworthy, *Preaching the Whole Bible as Christian Scripture*, p. 135-244; Dan McCartney and Charles Clayton, *Let the Reader Understand*, p. 223-242; R. C. Sproul, *Knowing Scripture*, p. 89-90, 94-99; Robert Stein, *A Basic Guide to Interpreting the Bible*, p. 73-202; William Klein, Craig Blomberg, and Robert Hubbard, Jr., *Introduction to Biblical Interpretation*, p. 323-448.

2. What is the historical situation?

To the extent possible, we must seek to discover and write notes about the following[9]:

1. Who is the author?
2. Where was the author at the time of this writing? What were his personal circumstances when he was writing?
3. Who were the readers?
4. Where were the readers? What were their personal circumstances at the time of the writing?
5. What was the author's purpose? Was he addressing certain problems? theological problems? relational problems? circumstantial problems?
6. What was the relationship between the author and the readers?
7. What can we discover about the social, political, economic, and cultural environment of the readers and of the author?

(In some cases, you will be asking these seven questions about a speaker and his listeners. For example, in studying the Sermon on the Mount, you will be asking these questions about Jesus and his listeners.)

Some preachers have asked, "What do I do if I don't have books that would provide me with historical information?" To this there is an encouraging reply. It is true that scholars have supplied some very helpful insights, but what is the primary source for their most important facts? It is the Bible itself. And how do we make these discoveries in the Bible?

- *We look first at the contents of the biblical book in which our passage occurs.* We want to always give close attention to the beginning and the end because this is often where we will find answers. However, we also want to search throughout the book.

- *We also turn to the historical books.* In the case of the New Testament epistles, we would look to Acts. In studying Philippians, where would we find helpful historical information? Acts 16. But what about the Old Testament? Let's consider, for example, Psalm 51. What is that psalm about? David's repentance. Where would you look for historical insights? 2 Samuel, chapters 11 and 12. Please look at the note at the heading of Psalm 51.

3. What comes before and after the biblical passage that I am studying?

We should carefully read the passages that precede and follow the passage that we are studying. By doing this, we enter into the author's flow of thought, and we are therefore able to more fully understand our passage.

We also want to consider the chapter, the book, and the testament in which the passage is found, and we must always keep in mind the teachings of the whole Bible.

Sometimes the author is actually serving as an editor who has collected various writings and sayings of others. For example, Luke did this when he wrote his Gospel and when he wrote Acts. In studying passages from those kinds of books, we read what comes before and after our passage, and we ask, "Why did the editor include this material at this point?"

---

9 You will find these questions (stated in similar ways) in all of the better works on Bible study methods. Personally, I am indebted to The Navigators who, in the early 1970's, first taught me the importance of searching for the answers to such questions.

Summary

When we study a Bible passage, *the first thing* we always do is study the context. We must resist the temptation to rush into a study of the content of the passage before we first give careful attention to the context: What kind of literature is this? What is the historical context? And what comes before and after the passage that I am studying? Studying the context always comes first!

Now let's look at an example. We are going to study the context of Philippians 4:4-9, and we will use the Bible as our only source. We will NOT break up into small groups at this point. As you make your discoveries, we will all write them down together.

Studying the Context
(Using the Bible as Your Only Source of Information)
Working an Example
Philippians 4:4-9

(**Note to teacher/facilitator:** Give each student a copy of the worksheet shown on p. 30, entitled "Studying the Context." While remaining together in your large group, have someone read Philippians 4:4-9. Then guide the students through the questions on the worksheet, allowing them to discover and share their answers with the entire group. In the notes below, the answers are provided. Do not simply give these answers. Help the students make discoveries, and have them write down the answers on their worksheets.)

1. **What kind of literature is this?** (Law, letter, parable, history, poetry, prophecy, proverbs, prayer, speech, apocalyptic writing, or some other form?)

   Philippians is a letter.

2. **What is the historical situation?**

   a) **Who is the author?**

   - The senders are Paul and Timothy. (Phil. 1:1)
   - The author is Paul. (Phil. 1:3 "I"; 1:4 "my"; 1:6 "I", and so on throughout the letter)
   - Paul was a Roman citizen. (Acts 16:37-39) He was God's special messenger to the Gentiles. (Acts 9:15) (Teacher/Facilitator: There is of course much more we could learn about the Apostle Paul from other Scriptures, but we will not pursue that information in this exercise.)

   b) **Where was the author at the time of this writing?** What were his personal circumstances as he was writing/speaking?

   - In prison (Phil. 1:7, 13)
   - Where was the prison? In Rome (Phil. 1:13 the "imperial guard"; 4:22 "Caesar's household")

   c) **Who are the readers?**

   - "all the saints . . . at Philippi, with the overseers and deacons" (Phil.1:1-2)
   - There were Gentiles in the congregation. For example, Lydia and her household (Acts 16:14-15) and the jailer and his household. (Acts 16:27-34)
   - There were Jews in the church, some of whom were trying to impose Old Testament ceremonial law on the Philippian believers. (Phil. 3:2-3)

   d) **Where were the readers?** What were their personal circumstances at the time of the writing?

   - Philippi (Phil. 1:1) – a Roman colony, a leading city in Macedonia (Acts 16:12)
   - They were suffering. (Phil. 1:28-30)
   - As already noted above, they were under pressure from certain Jews in the congregation to observe Old Testament ceremonial laws. (Phil. 3:2-3)

e) **What was the author's purpose?** Was he addressing certain problems? theological problems? relational problems? circumstantial problems?

- **General purposes** – 1) To express his thanksgiving, joy, and confidence in Christ's workings in and through them as well as his own great affection for them (Phil. 1:3-8); 2) To communicate his gratitude for their generosity toward him (4:15-17); 3) To urge them to experience joy at all times (4:4; also "joy" is mentioned throughout the letter)
- **Relational problems** – 1) Improperly motivated preachers (1:15); 2) Lack of unity (1:27, 2:2, 4:2-3); 3); Worry about Epaphroditus (2:25-30)
- **Theological problems** – Legalism imposed by the Judaizers (3:1-11)

f) **What do I know about the relationship between the author and the readers?**

From the Letter to the Philippians

- Paul prayed for them all the time with thanksgiving in his heart and with confidence in God's work in their lives. He had deep affection for them. (1:3-8)
- Paul was hoping to send Timothy to them soon. He himself was also hoping to visit them soon. (2:23-24)
- Paul speaks of some of them as being his fellow workers in ministry. (4:2-3)
- The Philippians had sent gifts to Paul when he was in need. (4:18)

From Acts 16:11 – Acts 17:1

- Paul and Silas were the missionaries to Philippi who saw the conversion of Lydia and her household at the birth of this church. (16:11-15)
- Paul and Silas were imprisoned because of their involvement in the deliverance of a slave girl from demon possession. (16-24)
- The Philippian jailer and his household were converted. (25-34)
- Paul and Silas were released from prison after which they went to Lydia's house and encouraged all of the believers before departing for Thessalonica. (16:35 –17:1)

g) **What can we discover about the social, political, economic, and cultural environment of the readers and of the author?**

- The readers and the author were living under Roman rule. (Phil. 1:13; 4:22)
- It was a time of persecution. (1:7, 13, 29-30)

3. **What comes before and after the biblical passage that I am studying?**

Immediately before? In Philippians 4:1-3, Paul is dealing with conflict between Euodia and Syntyche. Such conflict was of course preventing them from rejoicing always.

Immediately after? In Philippians 4:10-19, Paul is expressing his gratitude for the generosity of the Philippians toward him. He also says that he has learned to be content in all circumstances. He has told them in vs. 6 that they should not be anxious, and in these verses, 10-19, he is declaring his own freedom from anxiety about the provision of his daily needs.

In the book? Throughout his letter to the Philippians, many times Paul mentions "joy." He does not want anything to prevent the Philippians from experiencing joy in Christ. In each chapter it is also obvious that he has a deep longing to see them making spiritual progress. He says it very plainly in chapter one, verse 25: "I know that I will remain and continue with you all, for your progress and joy in the faith."

In the testament in which our passage is found? The joy of Christ is a major theme of the entire New Testament. In John 16:22, Jesus said to His disciples, ". . . your hearts will rejoice, and no one will take your joy from you." In verse 24 of that same chapter, He says, "Ask, and you will receive, that your joy may be full."

In the whole Bible? Joy is a theme that is seen throughout the Bible. In both the Old and New Testaments, we see that we were made to experience joy in our relationship with God. In Psalm 35:9, David says, "Then my soul will rejoice in the Lord, exulting in his salvation." In Isaiah 61:10, the prophet says, "I will greatly rejoice in the Lord, my soul shall exult in my God." In Revelation 19:7, we find that this will ever be a major theme in the hearts of God's people. The great multitude in heaven says, "Let us rejoice and exult and give him the glory, for the marriage of the Lamb has come, and his Bride has made herself ready."

LECTURE TWO
STUDYING THE CONTENT
Four Action Steps

Having studied the context of the passage, we are now ready to analyze the content. There are four major steps in studying the content:

1) Read the passage again and again, and pray.
2) Write notes on the details.
3) Write the outline.
4) Write the main idea.

1. READ THE PASSAGE AGAIN AND AGAIN, AND PRAY.

- **Read the passage again and again.**

  John Stott says, "Read the text, re-read it, re-read it, and read it again. Turn it over and over in your mind . . . . Probe your text, like a bee with a spring blossom, or like a hummingbird probing a hibiscus flower for its nectar. Worry at it like a dog with a bone. Suck it as a child sucks an orange. Chew it as a cow chews the cud."[10]

  As we read, we must constantly ask, "What is the author (or speaker) saying to his readers (or listeners)?" We are looking for the author's main idea. Sometimes, but not often, the author will clearly state his main idea. When he does, we often see it at the beginning or the end of the passage, and sometimes he reveals his central thought through repetition. However, in most cases, we will not discover the main idea until we have carefully studied the details of all of the verses in the passage.

  We also ask, *"What is the author (or speaker) saying about what he is saying?"* That is, what are the primary points he is making about his main idea?[11] We are looking for the structure of his message, i.e. we are looking for the way in which the verses might group together. We are trying to understand the flow of the passage.

- **As we read, we must continue to pray.**

  John Stott says, "Speaking personally, I have always found it helpful to do as much of my sermon preparation as possible on my knees, with the Bible open before me, in prayerful study."[12]

  We must humbly pray for understanding, as the Psalmist did in Psalm 119:18, "Open my eyes that I may behold wondrous things out of your law."

  We read, and we pray, as we think about what the author is saying. However, we do not yet write down the outline and main idea. We must first study the details.

---

10 John Stott, p. 220.
11 Haddon Robinson, p. 40.
12 Ibid, p. 222.

2. **WRITE NOTES ON THE DETAILS.**

We carefully study each verse, starting at the beginning of the passage and working all the way through to the end. For each verse, we do the following six things:

1) **Identify the VERBS.**

Verbs include *action* words such as run, preach, pray, repent, help, give, baptize, and send. Verbs also include *being* words such as am, is, are, was, were, will be.

The verbs in a verse will guide you into the author's (or speaker's) meaning, as they will help you to see the phrases in each sentence.[13]

2) **Locate the CENTRAL PHRASE.**

In the central phrase, the author (speaker) is giving the primary thought of the verse. Write down this central phrase. Use the exact words given in the verse.

3) **List the KEY WORDS.**

Examples: Romans 5:10 – "reconciled", "saved"; Ephesians 2:8-9 – "grace", "faith", "gift", "works"; Psalm 51:1 – "mercy", "steadfast love", "transgressions"

4) **Look for LINKING WORDS.**

These are words that connect the thoughts of this verse to other verses (see Romans 8:1) and words that connect thoughts within the verse itself (see Romans 8:7). The following are some examples of linking words: therefore, since, because, if, on the other hand, however, but, also, finally, in addition, for, and in view of.

5) **Ask, "WHAT QUESTIONS IS THE AUTHOR ANSWERING FOR HIS READERS IN THIS VERSE?"**

In each verse, the author is answering at least one of the following six questions:*How, what, why, when, where, and who?* In fact, in all communication, one or more of these questions is being answered.

After you write down all of the questions the author is answering, then determine which of these is the **primary question** he is answering in the verse you are studying. The author's primary question is answered in the central phrase of the sentence.

6) **Ask, "WHAT QUESTIONS DO I HAVE ABOUT THIS VERSE? AND WHAT QUESTIONS MIGHT THOSE IN THE CONGREGATION HAVE?"** (Use the six questions: how, what, why, when, where, and who.)

You will not have time in your seminar workshops to provide the answers to the questions that you have (or those your congregation might have) about each verse. You will only have time to write down a few of the questions. When you are actually preparing to preach, <u>you will of course write down your answers</u> to those questions and use much of that material in your sermon.

---

13   It was Chris Wright whom I first heard call for close attention to the verbs which will guide us into meaning. Also, Howard and Bill Hendricks say, "Verbs are critical. They're the action words that tell us who is doing what." (*Living By the Book*, p. 116)

Complete the previous six steps for each verse. <u>After</u> you have applied those six steps to all of the verses in your passage, then go back to the beginning of your passage and search for other things such as the following:

- **Definitions** – e.g., Hebrews 11:1, "Now faith is the assurance of things hoped for, the conviction of things not seen."
- **Lists** – e.g., 1 Timothy 3:1-7 provides a list of the qualifications of an elder.
- **Contrasts** – (things that are different) – e.g., Romans 8:5, "those who live according to the flesh" and "those who live according to the Spirit."
- **Comparisons** – (things that are the same or similar) – e.g., Eph. 5:25, "Husbands, love your wives, as Christ loved the Church and gave Himself up for her."
- **Cause and effect** – e.g., 1 Kings 11:9, "And the Lord was angry with Solomon, because his heart had turned away from the Lord, the God of Israel . . . ."
- **Metaphors (picture words)** – e.g., Psalm 1 says that the blessed man will be "like a tree planted by streams of water that yields its fruit in its season, and its leaf does not wither." Also, Matthew 5:14, "You are the light of the world."
- **Surprises**[14] – Does this verse present something that is very surprising in view of what was said in the verse(s) just before it? e.g., Acts 20:29-30
- **Great themes of the Bible** – e.g., the kingdom of God, justification, sanctification, true righteousness, redemption, the atonement, forgiveness, grace, love, etc.
- **Cross-references** – other Bible references that improve our understanding of verses in this passage or that further establish our appreciation of the importance of a particular concept.

VERY IMPORTANT: As you study the details, **TAKE LOTS OF NOTES.** Your notes will provide the information that you will need in discovering and writing the outline and the main idea of the passage.

Example – Please turn to Acts 1:8 as we will take <u>the first six steps</u> in analyzing the details of a verse. Please make your own notes as we work together. [Note to teacher/facilitator: You should allow the students (or seminar delegates) to make their discoveries through open discussion with the whole group (not in workshop groups) at this point. Workshop groups will be held at a later point in your seminar. Also, please remember that although the answers are given in the lecture notes below, you will not want to give them the answers. Instead, please guide them point by point in their discussion so that they arrive at the answers. In number 6 below, you will find that they will possibly come up with questions that are not included here. This should be an exciting time of discovery for them.]

1. **Verbs** – will receive, has come, will be (Remember that the verbs guide you into meaning.)
2. **Central phrase** – "you will be my witnesses"
3. **Key words** – power, the Holy Spirit, witnesses
4. **Linking words** – But
5. **What questions are being answered by the author/speaker for his readers/listeners?**
   - What will they become? "you will be my witnesses"
   - How will they be witnesses? "you will receive power"
   - When will they receive this power? "when the Holy Spirit has come upon you"
   - Where will they be witnesses? "in Jerusalem and in all Judea and Samaria, and to the end of the earth."

---

14 I learned to look for surprises from Chris Wright.

6. What questions do I have? And what questions might those in the congregation have?
- Who is the Holy Spirit?
- When does a Christian receive the Holy Spirit?
- What does it mean to be a witness?
- Why does Jesus place Jerusalem, Judea, Samaria, and the end of the earth in this order?

<u>An important reminder to the students or seminar delegates:</u> The questions you have listed under step 6 (above) are necessary for your further analysis of the verse. As we have mentioned before, when you are actually preparing for a sermon, you will need to go back to these questions so that you can study them and write down the answers to each question <u>in your notebook</u>. You will use these answers in explaining the text to the people of your congregation.

Now let's work a second example. Please turn to Matthew 28:19-20, and we will again "write notes on the details." We will study these two verses together.

1. **Verbs (all action and being words, including participles)** – go, make, baptizing, teaching, observe, commanded, am
2. **Central phrase** – "Go therefore and make disciples"
3. **Key words** – disciples, nations, Father, Son, Holy Spirit, age
4. **Linking words** – therefore, and
5. **What questions are being answered by the author/speaker for his readers/listeners?**
   - What shall they do? "Go . . . and make disciples"
   - Of whom? "of all nations"
   - How? (or What? What will be involved?) "Baptizing them" and "teaching them"
   - In what name? "in the name of the Father and of the Son and of the Holy Spirit"
   - What must they teach them? "to observe all that I have commanded you"
   - Who would be with them? Jesus said, "I am with you."
   - How long would He be with them? "always, to the end of the age"
6. **What questions do I have? And what questions might those in the congregation have?**
   - What is a disciple?
   - Who are the nations?
   - When should the disciples go?
   - Why does Jesus say "in the name of the Father and the Son and the Holy Spirit"?
   - What is the relationship between the Father, Son, and Holy Spirit?
   - What are the things that Jesus commanded the apostles to teach?
   - How is Jesus with us always?
   - When will the "end of the age" come?

<u>Please remember</u> that in addition to the six steps you have just taken with Acts 1:8 and Matthew 28:19-20, you will also write down other important observations (definitions, lists, contrasts, comparisons, cause and effect, metaphors, surprises, great themes of the Bible, and cross references). In your workshop groups, you will search for those things as well.

3. WRITE THE OUTLINE.

This outline of the passage is called the exegetical outline. How do we go about writing it?

- **Identify the "thought units," i.e., the verse groupings.**

  What do we mean by "thought units"[15] or verse groupings? These are the verses that are working together in making one point.

  As you read through your passage, one verse after another, ask yourself, "Is the author still talking about the same point in this verse that he was talking about in the previous verse?" Which verses go together? You are looking to see how the verses should be grouped.

  In longer passages, these thought units will be paragraphs. In shorter passages, these thought units will be verses or sentences. In very long passages, such as those found in the narrative portions of Scripture, the thought units will sometimes include many verses..

  To discover the thought units (or verse groupings), continue to read the text carefully and _look at your personal "notes on the details."_ Study those notes that you have written on each verse in which you identified 1) the verbs, 2) the central phrase, 3) the key words, 4) the linking words, and, most importantly, 5) "What questions is the author answering for his readers in this verse?" – how, what, why, when, where, and who.

  As you begin to discover what you believe to be the thought units or verse groupings, notice how each thought unit relates to the preceding and following thought unit. _What is the flow of thought?_

  The Number of Thought Units: You may find your number of thought units (or verse groupings) to be reducible to a smaller number. For example, initially you may be dealing with five or six, but then you may see that two or more can be combined.

- **Write the central idea of each thought unit (group of verses) in one complete sentence.**

  These sentences _are the main points in your outline of the passage_, i.e. _the exegetical outline._ (Include corresponding verse numbers for each point.)

  Remember that in each thought unit (verse grouping) the author is providing an answer to at least one of the six questions for his audience: how, what, why, when, where, and who? _Write down the author's answer in one clear, concise, complete sentence._

- **Write the sub-points in complete sentences.** (Include verse numbers.)

  Each sub-point is directly related to the central idea of that thought unit. _Look at your "notes on the details" to discover these sub-points._ In each sub-point, answers to the six questions – how, what, why, when, where, and who – are being given about the central idea of that thought unit.

- **Write each point in the past tense and use proper nouns where appropriate.**

---

15   Haddon Robinson, p. 54-55.

4. **WRITE THE MAIN IDEA.**

- **The main idea is to be written in <u>one complete sentence</u>, using past tense verbs and proper nouns.**

- **Use the six questions (how, what, why, when, where, and who?) in making your discovery.** The author is answering one of the six questions for his readers.

- **Sometimes the main idea is clearly given in the text.** Often it is found at the beginning and/or at the end of a passage, and sometimes it is given through repetition. Let's look at two texts where the main idea is clearly given. **(Note to teachers/facilitators:** Have the students work with you through these texts. Let them make the discoveries.)

   ◆ **Genesis 1**

   Look at the beginning of the chapter and at the end. Then look for repetition throughout the chapter.

   Which of the six questions was Moses answering for the people of Israel? He is answering the question "How?" – "How did the world come into being?"

   So what is the main idea? Moses was telling the people of Israel that God created the world by His spoken word.

   ◆ **James 1:19-25**

   What question was James answering for the scattered Jewish Christians? James was answering the question "What?" – "What must they do with the Word of God?"

   What is the main idea? James was telling the scattered Jewish Christians that they must be doers of the Word and not simply hearers.

- **Often the main idea is not explicitly stated in the text, and it must be discovered by looking carefully at the main points of your outline of the passage.**

As you look at all of <u>the *main* points</u> in your outline, keep asking yourself three questions: "What question was the author answering? What was the author saying to his readers? How can this be written in one complete sentence?"

Philippians 2:1-11 is an example of a passage in which we discover the main idea by looking carefully at the main points of the outline of the passage. Let's work together through that text.

DISCOVERING THE MAIN IDEA
Working Through An Example
Philippians 2:1-11

(Note to teachers/facilitators: Have the students work through the following passage with you (not in workshop groups at this point). Read the passage with them. Then help them make the discoveries. Guide them to the outline and main idea given below. Explain to them that you will only be looking for the main points of the outline and not the sub-points.)

The Main Points of the Outline

   I.   Paul told the Philippians that they should be unified. (vs. 1-2)

  II.   Paul told them to relate to one another with humility. (vs. 3-4)

III.   Paul exhorted them to follow Jesus' example of humility. (vs. 5-11)

Discovering the Main Idea

What was Paul saying to the Philippians? _What question_ was he answering for them?

Paul was answering the question "What?" – "What must they do about the problem of division and conflict among themselves?"

So what is the main idea?

It could be stated in several ways. But here is one way in which it might be written:

Paul was telling the Philippians to be unified by following Jesus' example of humility as they relate to one another.

REVIEWING THE ACTION STEPS
In Studying the Bible Passage

Studying the Context: Three Action Steps

When we open our Bible to study a passage, we always give <u>first</u> consideration to context. We write down the answers to the following three questions:

1)   What kind of literature is this?

2)   What is the historical situation?

3)   What comes before and after this biblical passage that is before me?

Studying the Content: Four Action Steps

<u>After</u> we have given attention to the context, then we study the content. These are our four action steps in studying the content of the passage:

1) Read the passage again and again, and pray.

2) Write notes on the details.

3) Write the outline.

4) Write the main idea.

PART TWO
Writing Your Sermon

LECTURE THREE
WRITING YOUR SERMON
Five Action Steps

We have worked on exegesis, i.e., we have studied the text in order to understand what the original author (or speaker) was saying to the people to whom he was writing (or speaking) at that time. We have read again and again and prayed; we have written notes on the details; we have written the outline; and we have written the main idea of the passage. We have worked hard to understand the author's message.

Now we move on to take that message to the people whom we are serving. We must build a bridge from the original author's world to the world of our listeners. This will require that we live in two worlds and that we engage in what John Stott has called "double listening." We listen to the Bible, and we listen to the world in which we and our listeners are living. In doing this, we are seeking to remain faithful to the message of the ancient biblical text while bringing that message to our listeners in a way that is clear to them and relevant to their context.[16]

There are five steps that we will follow in writing our sermons:

1. Write the theme statement of the sermon.
2. Write the outline.
3. Re-write the outline and fill in the details (explanations, illustrations, and applications).
4. Write the introduction.
5. Write the conclusion.

1. WRITE THE THEME STATEMENT OF YOUR SERMON.

- **We write this central theme in one clear, concise, complete sentence.**

- **How do we develop this theme statement? How do we write this one sentence?**

  We look at the main idea of the Bible passage (Side A), and we bring that idea <u>into the present as we write the theme statement of the sermon</u> (Side B). We use <u>present tense verbs</u>, and we use <u>personal pronouns</u> (I, we, us, you) when writing our theme statement (Side B).[17] Here are a few examples:

  ◆ **Matthew 7:15-20**

    Main Idea (Side A) <u>Jesus warned His disciples</u> to beware of false prophets who would come to <u>them</u> in sheep's clothing but would actually be ravenous wolves. (past tense)

    Theme Statement (Side B) <u>Jesus warns us</u> to beware of false prophets who come to <u>us</u> in sheep's clothing but are actually ravenous wolves. (present tense)

---

16   John Stott, p. 137-144.
17   Walter C. Kaiser, Jr., *Preaching and Teaching from the Old Testament*, p. 57-58.

♦ **James 1:19-25**

Main Idea (Side A) <u>James was telling the scattered Jewish Christians</u> that <u>they</u> must be doers of the Word and not simply hearers. (past tense)

Theme Statement (Side B) <u>You and I must be</u> doers of the Word and not simply hearers. (present tense)

♦ **Jeremiah 23:16-32**

Main Idea (Side A) <u>God was warning His people</u> not to listen to those false prophets who were preaching their own visions and dreams and leading the people further into sin. (past tense)

Theme Statement (Side B) <u>You and I must not listen</u> to the dream preachers! (present tense)

Sometimes we may become creative in developing our theme statements. We may write them in ways that are more contemporary and appropriate to our particular listeners. Also, our theme statements (Side B) may sometimes be a bit shorter than the main idea of the passage (Side A), but we must be sure that the theme statement (Side B) is clearly presenting the exact same thought that is given in the main idea of the passage (Side A).

The careful development of the theme statement of your sermon is essential. A great preacher named J. H. Jowett said, "I have a conviction that no sermon is ready for preaching . . . until we can express its theme in a short . . . sentence as clear as a crystal. I find the getting of that sentence is the hardest, the most exacting and the most fruitful labor in my study. . . ." [18]

2. **WRITE THE OUTLINE OF YOUR SERMON.**

   • **What is the purpose of an outline?**[19]

      - It helps the congregation follow the flow of your sermon and remember its content.

      - It helps you as a preacher in your preparation.

         a) It provides an orderly structure for the writing of your sermon.
         b) It helps you see where you will place your explanations, illustrations, and applications.

   • **The sermon outline should be written in <u>clear</u>, <u>concise</u>, <u>complete</u> sentences.**

      Dr. Haddon Robinson says, "Since each point in a sermon represents an idea, it should be a grammatically complete sentence. When words or phrases stand as points, they deceive us because they are incomplete and vague."[20]

---

18   J. H. Jowett, quoted in John Stott's *Between Two Worlds*, p. 226.
19   Dr. Bryan Chapell refers to the outline as a "mental map for all to follow" in *Christ-Centered Preaching*. See his comments on the value of the outline for the preacher and for the listeners on p. 130-31.
20   Haddon Robinson, p. 131.

- **The outline should be written in the present tense.**

  The sermon outline should use terms that make it clear that we are speaking to the people before us about their lives and that we are not simply telling them about other people who lived long ago. In order to do this, we must remember the following:[21]

  - **Avoid all use of proper names in the outline except for the names of God.** Our sermon outline is not about the people and places of thousands of years ago. It is about the people who are listening to you.

  - **In the sermon outline, do not use past tense verbs; use the present tense.** This sermon is to those who are now living.

  - **In the sermon outline, do not use third person pronouns** (they, them, it, she, and he). Instead, use first and second person pronouns (we, you and I, and us). Sometimes we may simply use the more direct "you", but we must be careful to do this with humility.

- **You may choose to add brief, memorable headings.** (In your workshops, focus on complete sentences. Memorable headings are <u>optional</u>.)

3. <u>RE-WRITE</u> YOUR OUTLINE AND FILL IN THE DETAILS OF YOUR SERMON.

- **LOOK BACK AT THE NOTES** you took when you were studying the details of the passage. Those notes will provide much of the information that you will include in the writing of your sermon. However, you will <u>not include ALL</u> of that information in your sermon. (See "Write Notes on the Details of Each Verse.")

- **ADD ILLUSTRATIONS.**

  - **Our sermons will include brief stories, examples, sayings, and comparisons.** These illustrations will help our listeners gain a better understanding of the passage.

  - **You should write out your illustrations completely.** By doing this, you will know how long they will be. Also, writing them out will help you to be more accurate and effective in all that you say.

  - **Be careful that your illustrations truly fit the meaning of the Bible passage.**

  - **Be sure that your illustrations are well chosen for your audience.** Consider their age, their education, and their cultural background.

  - **What are the sources of our illustrations?** Our first source is the Bible itself. We can illustrate a truth taught in one Bible passage with a story from another part of the Bible. In addition to the Bible, we have history, biographies, novels, short stories, newspapers, our own experiences, and other sources.

---

21 Kaiser, p. 57-58.

- **How many illustrations should we have? How long should they be?** We should be careful that we do not have too many and that they are not too long. Our illustrations should cause the Scripture to shine more brightly before us. We want our listeners to understand and remember the message of the Bible.

- **ALWAYS INCLUDE APPLICATIONS.**

  - **We must ask, "What difference does it make to us and to our listeners?"**
  - **We should try to have personal applications throughout our sermons.**
  - **We must apply the message to ourselves.** We must be like Ezra who "set his heart" to "practice" what he studied and taught. (Ezra 7:10, NASB)

  The following is a helpful application tool by the Navigators (with slight modifications):[22]

  - **Is there a SIN for me to avoid? or confess?**
  - **Is there a PROMISE from God for me to claim?**
  - **Is there an EXAMPLE for me to follow? or not to follow?**
  - **Is there a COMMAND for me to obey?**
  - **Is there KNOWLEDGE for me to understand and remember?** (Knowledge about God, the church, individual believers, unbelievers, etc.)

  (When teaching in English, it might be helpful to make mention of the acronym SPECK – Sin, Promise, Example, Command, Knowledge. In other languages, this acronym is of course of no value.)

4. **WRITE THE INTRODUCTION.**

   - **The purpose of the introduction is to "create interest and convince the listener that he can be helped by hearing your message."[23]**

   - **The introduction should prepare your congregation for the central theme of your sermon.**

     This can be done by including our sermon theme statement, or it can be done in less direct ways. In any case, the introduction should be directly tied to the central theme of your sermon.

   - **It should not be too long.**

     If our introduction is too long, our listeners may not be willing to go on and listen to our sermon. They will stop listening!

     A great preacher once said, "As a rule, don't make the introduction too long. It is always a pity to build a great porch to a little house."[24]

   - **It is usually written after the body of the sermon has been completed.**

     We want to build the house before we build the porch. Otherwise, we might find ourselves trying to make the house fit the porch rather than fitting the porch to the house.

---

22 *The Navigator Bible Studies Handbook,* p. 23.
23 Warren and David Wiersbe, *The Elements of Preaching,* p. 75.
24 C. H. Spurgeon, *Lectures to My Students,* p. 143.

5. WRITE THE CONCLUSION

- **Clearly focus on the central theme of the sermon ("the big idea."[25]).**

- **The conclusion should not be too long.**

- **You may sometimes include a recapitulation of your main points and a restatement of your central theme.**

- <u>**There must be a call for a response to the primary message of the text.**</u> We must help the men, the women, and the children of our congregations to apply the message to their lives. There are times when this will involve a pleading with the souls who are before us. As one preacher has said, "It is a tragedy to see pastors state the facts and sit down. Good preaching pleads with people to respond to the Word of God."[26]

---

25 The "Big Idea" is the term that Haddon Robinson has used in referring to the primary point of a sermon.
26 John Piper, *The Supremacy of God in Preaching*, p. 95.

REVIEWING THE ACTION STEPS
In Writing Your Sermon

1. Write the theme statement of the sermon.

2. Write the outline.

3. Re-write the outline and fill in the details (explanations, illustrations, and applications).

4. Write the introduction.

5. Write the conclusion.

WRITING A MANUSCRIPT OF YOUR SERMON AND PRAYING OVER IT

There are two final very important matters that we must address: the writing of a full manuscript of your sermon and then praying over it.

- **WRITING A MANUSCRIPT OF YOUR SERMON**

  Writing a complete manuscript of our sermons is extremely valuable to us as preachers. It helps us to be accurate in the expression of our thoughts as we carefully choose our words. It also helps us to manage the amount of time that we will give to each part of the sermon when we actually deliver it to the people.

  After we have written our sermon, we should read our manuscript over and over again in private. We want to imprint the words on our minds and our hearts. Some of us have found that reading our sermons out loud can be very beneficial. Sometimes this verbal reading will help us to realize that what we have written is not clear. Also, we may recognize that we have used the same words too often or that we have repeated certain ideas in a way that is not helpful. We can then make the necessary corrections.

  When the time comes for you to preach, there are two ways that you can effectively use your written sermon:

  1) Take your manuscript with you, but arrange your text and highlight or underline key words and phrases in such a way that you do not read it. It is very helpful if this manuscript is written within the structure of an outline.

  2) Take a detailed outline of your sermon with you. The notes included in this outline should be very well organized, very clear, very complete. They should also include your transitions, i.e., your sentences that serve as bridges from one point to the next. Those <u>transitions should be fully written out</u> in your notes.

- **PRAYING OVER YOUR SERMON**

  We should always pray over our messages. John Stott offers these words concerning the extreme importance of our preparation in prayer:

  It is on our knees before the Lord that we can make the message our own, possess or re-possess it until it possesses us. Then, when we preach it, it will come neither from our notes, nor from our memory, but out of the depths of our own conviction, as an authentic utterance of our heart. . . . .We need to pray until our text comes freshly alive to us, the glory shines forth from it, the fire burns in our heart, and we begin to experience the explosive power of God's Word within us. . . . . The pressure begins to build up inside us, until we feel we can contain it no longer. It is then that we are ready to preach.[27]

John Stott, p. 258.

WORKSHOP GROUPS

NOTES TO TEACHERS/FACILITATORS

Teachers and facilitators, it would be helpful to divide into workshop groups at this point and have the students/delegates apply what they have learned.

Worksheets: Please be sure that each delegate has an unused copy of the four worksheets listed below.

1) **Studying the Context** (If you choose a passage from Philippians, then you and the delegates will have already completed this work together. However, if you choose a passage from some other book of the Bible, the delegates will need to use the worksheet on p. 30 and write down their discoveries.)

2) **Write Notes on the Details of Each Verse** (It is important that you as the teacher/facilitator see the instructions given at the bottom of this worksheet on p. 31 and <u>read them to the students/delegates</u>.)

3) **Side <u>A</u> – The Outline and Main Idea of the Biblical Passage** (p. 32)

4) **Side <u>B</u> – Theme Statement and Outline of Your Sermon** (p. 33)

Suggested passages: On p. 36, you will find some suggested passages for your workshops.

STUDYING THE CONTEXT

1. **What kind of literature is this?** (Law, letter, parable, history, poetry, prophecy, proverbs, prayer, speech, apocalyptic writing, or some other form?)

2. **What is the historical situation?**

   a) Who is the author (speaker)?

   b) Where was the author (speaker) at the time of this writing? What were his personal circumstances as he was writing/speaking?

   c) Who are the readers (listeners)?

   d) Where were the readers (listeners)? What were their personal circumstances at the time of the writing/speaking?

   e) What is the author's (speaker's) purpose? Was he addressing certain problems? theological problems? relational problems? circumstantial problems?

   f) What do we know about the relationship between the author (speaker) and the readers (listeners)? Is there anything that we can learn about that relationship from the book in which our passage appears? or from some other book of the Bible?

   g) What can we discover about the social, political, economic, and cultural environment of the readers and of the author?

3. **What comes before and after the biblical passage that I am studying?**

(Use the back of this sheet as needed to write answers to any of the above questions. In your future studies, if you do not have copies of this form, please consider hand-writing the questions and your answers.)

WRITE NOTES ON THE DETAILS OF EACH VERSE

Vs. _____

1) **Verbs**

2) **Central phrase**

3) **Key words**

4) **Linking words**

5) **What questions are being answered by the author/speaker for his readers/listeners? (How, what, why, when, where, and who?)**

6) **What questions do I have? And what questions might those in the congregation have? (How, what, why, when, where, and who?)**

Vs. _____

1) **Verbs**

2) **Central phrase**

3) **Key words**

4) **Linking words**

5) **What questions are being answered by the author/speaker for his readers/listeners? (How, what, why, when, where, and who?)**

6) **What questions do I have? And what questions might those in the congregation have? (How, what, why, when, where, and who?)**

Notes: 1) <u>Please hand-write the above form on your own blank sheets of paper in studying each verse in your Bible passage.</u> In the study of various forms of biblical literature (for example, history, parables, laws, and proverbs), your process will be a bit different. However, this approach to verse by verse analysis will be applicable to many passages that you will study. **2) After completing the 6 steps in analyzing each verse** (as shown above), then study all of the verses in the passage and write down definitions, lists, contrasts, comparisons, cause and effect, metaphors, surprises, great themes of the Bible, and cross-references.

SIDE A – THE OUTLINE AND MAIN IDEA OF THE BIBLICAL PASSAGE

Bible Reference: _____

The Outline of the Passage: **What did the author say *about* what he was saying? What did he say about his main idea?** Please use complete sentences to state what the author said. This will often, but not always, include words that come directly from the biblical text. Although four Roman numerals are provided below, you may have more or fewer main points. The number of main points will of course vary depending upon the passage you are studying. Also, you may wish to add sub-points, A, B, C, and 1, 2, 3, etc. On these sub-points, please use complete sentences and write the corresponding verse numbers at the end of each sentence. Remember that you are writing what the author said to his listeners.

I. (Vs. _____)

II. (Vs. _____)

III. (Vs. _____)

IV. (Vs. _____)

Main Idea of the Passage: What was the biblical author/speaker saying to his listeners at that time? Please answer this question in one clear, concise, and complete sentence. You may want to include the name of the biblical author/speaker and his listener(s) in this statement. For example, Moses was telling (or warning, reminding, encouraging, etc.) the children of Israel . . . .

_____

_____

_____

SIDE B – THE THEME STATEMENT AND OUTLINE OF YOUR SERMON

Bible Reference: ————————————————————————

The Theme Statement of Your Sermon: **What are you going to say to your audience?** Please answer this question in <u>one clear, concise, *complete* sentence</u> that is in the <u>present tense</u> and uses <u>personal pronouns</u>.

————————————————————————————————

————————————————————————————————

————————————————————————————————

Your Sermon Outline: **What are you going to say about what you are saying? What are you going to say about the idea you have expressed in the theme statement above?** <u>Please use complete sentences</u>. (You may add memorable brief phrases that will be helpful to your listeners. However, please give complete sentences first.) Although four Roman numerals are provided below, you may have more or fewer main points. The number of main points will of course vary depending upon the passage from which you are preaching. Also, you may wish to add sub-points, A, B, C, etc. On these sub-points, please use complete sentences. This will assure your clear statement of the idea that you are communicating from each section of the passage. Please make note of the verse numbers that relate to each sub-point.

I. (Vs. ————)

II. (Vs. ————)

III. (Vs. ————)

IV. (Vs. ————)

STUDYING THE BIBLE PASSAGE
(SIDE A)

STUDYING THE CONTEXT: Three Action Steps

Write answers to the following:

1. What kind of literature is this?
2. What is the historical situation?
3. What comes before and after the biblical passage that I am studying?

STUDYING THE CONTENT: Four Action Steps

1. **READ THE PASSAGE AGAIN AND AGAIN, AND PRAY.**
2. **WRITE NOTES ON THE DETAILS OF EACH VERSE.**

   - Identify the verbs.
   - Locate the central phrase.
   - List the key words.
   - Look for the linking words.
   - Ask, "What questions is the author answering for his readers?" Use the six questions: How? What? Why? When? Where? Who?
   - Ask, "What questions do I have (or might the congregation have) about this verse?" Again use the six questions: How? What? Why? When? Where? Who?

   After completing these steps for each verse, then look for definitions, lists, contrasts, comparisons, cause and effect, metaphors, surprises, great themes of the Bible, and cross-references.

3. WRITE THE OUTLINE.

   - Identify the "thought units", i.e. the verse groupings.
   - Write the central idea of each thought unit (group of verses) in one complete sentence.
   - Write the sub-points in complete sentences. (Include verse numbers.)
   - Write each point in the past tense and use proper nouns where appropriate.

4. WRITE THE MAIN IDEA.

   - Use the six questions (how, what, why, when, where, and who?) in making your discovery.
   - Sometimes the main idea is clearly stated in the text.
   - Often the main idea is not explicitly stated, but must be discovered by looking carefully at the main points of your outline of the passage.
   - Write the main idea in one complete sentence, using past tense verbs and proper nouns.

WRITING YOUR SERMON
(SIDE B)

Five Action Steps:

1. **WRITE THE THEME STATEMENT OF THE SERMON.**

2. **WRITE THE OUTLINE OF YOUR SERMON.**

   - Avoid all use of proper names in the outline except for the names of God.
   - In the sermon outline, do not use past tense verbs; use the present tense.
   - In the sermon outline, do not use third person pronouns. (Don't use "they", "them", "she", and "he". Instead, use "we", "you", and "I".)

   (You may choose to add brief, memorable headings.)

3. **RE-WRITE YOUR OUTLINE AND FILL IN THE DETAILS OF YOUR SERMON.**

   - Add explanations and cross references. (See your personal study notes.)
   - Add illustrations.
   - Add applications.

        S – Is there a **SIN** to confess?
        P – Is there a **PROMISE** to claim?
        E – Is there an **EXAMPLE** for me to follow? or not to follow?
        C – Is there a **COMMAND** to obey?
        K – Is there **KNOWLEDGE** to be understood and remembered?[28]

4. **WRITE THE INTRODUCTION.**

5. **WRITE THE CONCLUSION.**

Having completed your writing, *pray over your sermon.*

John Stott says, "It is on our knees before the Lord that we can make the message our own, possess or re-possess it until it possesses us. Then, when we preach it, it will come neither from our notes, nor from our memory, but out of the depths of our own conviction, as an authentic utterance of our heart. . . . . We need to pray until our text comes freshly alive to us, the glory shines forth from it, the fire burns in our heart, and we begin to experience the explosive power of God's Word within us. . . . . The pressure begins to build up inside us, until we feel we can contain it no longer. It is then that we are ready to preach."

---

28 Adapted from *The Navigator Bible Studies Handbook*, p. 23.

A FEW SUGGESTED PASSAGES
FOR WORKSHOP GROUPS

It is very important that the teacher/facilitator has selected the passages for the workshops in advance and done his own personal study. He should have completed all of the work according to the four instruments provided: Study the Context, Write Notes on the Details, Side A "The Outline and Main Idea of the Passage," and Side B "The Theme Statement and Outline of Your Sermon."

The following are a few suggested passages. The important thing is that you choose passages that are not too long and can be outlined fairly easily so that the delegates/students do not become discouraged.

New Testament

James 1:5-8
1 Peter 2:9-12
1 Peter 5:1-5
Colossians 4:2-6
Philippians 1:12-26
Philippians 2:1-11
Philippians 4:4-9
Ephesians 2:1-10
Romans 12:1-2
2 Timothy 4:1-8
1 Thessalonians 2:1-12
Matthew 5:13-16

Old Testament

Psalm 1
Psalm 32:1-5
Jeremiah 1:1-10
Isaiah 6:1-8 (Although the remainder of this chapter, i.e., verses 9-13, is a continuation of this encounter between Isaiah and God, you will probably not want to include those verses in your workshop. Doing an outline only on verses 1-8 will be much more manageable for your delegates/students.)

APPENDIX 1

EXAMPLES OF SERMON THEME STATEMENTS AND SIDE B OUTLINES
For Teachers/Facilitators

On the following pages (pp. 38-43) are some examples of sermon theme statements and outlines (Side B). If you select any of these texts for your workshops, you will not want to give copies of these examples to the delegates/students until AFTER they do their own work and have made their presentations. You will notice that verse numbers are given after every point, both main points and sub-points. This is to provide assurance that each part of the outline is drawn directly from the Bible passage on which the sermon is to be written.

As mentioned before, memorable headings may be added for the main points of your sermon outline. However, in these examples, we will not include such headings. We want to emphasize the fact that clear, concise, complete sentences are essential to your sermon outline.

Philippians 1:12-26

Theme Statement: God is bringing forth His good purposes in all of your difficult circumstances.

I. **God will use your difficult circumstances for the advancement of the Gospel.** (vs. 12-18)

   A. God will provide opportunities for you to tell people about Jesus in the midst of every difficult circumstance. (vs. 13)
   B. God will use your difficult circumstances to give boldness to others to preach the Gospel. (vs. 14)
   C. God will use wrongly motivated preachers, including those who hurt you personally, to proclaim His Gospel. (vs. 15-18)

II. **God will use your difficult circumstances to bring about your personal spiritual progress.** (vs. 19-21)

III. **For as long as God leaves you in this world, you can expect that He will lead you into fruitful service among His people.** (vs. 22-26)

   A. As you grow in love for Christ, you will be torn between the desire to be with Christ and the desire to remain here to serve Christ's people. (vs. 22-24)
   B. As you minister to God's people, you should be hopeful they will make progress in their joy and faith. (vs. 25-26)

Philippians 2:1-11

Theme Statement: You are to be unified by following Jesus' example of humility.

I.   **You are to be unified.** (vs. 1-2)

    A. You have all of the spiritual resources you need to be unified. (vs. 1)
       1. You have "encouragement in Christ." (vs. 1)
       2. You have "comfort from love." (vs. 1)
       3. You have "participation in the Spirit." (vs. 1)
       4. You have "affection and sympathy." (vs. 1)

    B. Your unity makes your pastors joyful. (vs. 2)

    C. You are to be one in every way. (vs. 2)
       1. You are to have the same thoughts toward one another. (vs. 2)
       2. You are to have the same love. (vs. 2)
       3. You are to be one in spirit. (vs. 2)
       4. You are to be focused on one purpose. (vs. 2)

II.   **You are to relate to one another with humility.** (vs. 3-4)

    A. You must be respectful of one another. (vs. 3)
    B. You must be considerate of one another's interests. (vs. 4)

III. **Our Lord Jesus is the supreme example that you and I must follow.** (vs. 5-11)

    A. Our Lord Jesus is God. (vs. 6; see also John 1:1; 17:5)
    B. Our Lord laid aside certain Divine privileges when He became a man. (vs. 6-7)
    C. Our Lord humbled Himself to the point of being hanged in the place of cursing that we deserved. (vs. 8; see also Galatians 3:31, Deuteronomy 21:22-23)
    D. God has exalted our Lord Jesus to the highest place. (vs. 9-11; see also 1 Peter 5:6)

Psalm 1

Theme Statement: We must choose the way of the godly man or woman who loves God's Word if we are to experience God's blessing.

I.   **We have been called to be godly men and women who love God's Word and are therefore greatly blessed.** (vs. 1-3)

    A.   We must avoid the influence of ungodly people. (vs. 1)
        1.   We must not listen to their counsel. (vs. 1; cf. 1 John 2:15-17)
        2.   We must not follow their path. (vs. 1)
        3.   We must not become one who leads others onto that pathway. (vs. 1; cf. Matt. 23:2)

    B.   We must saturate our lives with the Word of God. (vs. 2)
        1.   We must delight in the Word. (vs. 2; cf. Jeremiah 15:16)
        2.   We must meditate on the Word. (vs.2; cf. Joshua 1:8)

    C.   As we listen obediently to God's Word, our lives will be greatly blessed. (vs. 3)
        1.   We will be secure: "like a tree planted" (vs. 3)
        2.   We will be nourished and refreshed: "by streams of water" (vs. 3)
        3.   We will be fruitful: "yields its fruit in its season" (vs. 3; cf. John 15:16a, 27)
        4.   We will be full of vitality in all circumstances: "its leaf does not wither" (vs. 3; cf. 2 Cor. 4:8-9)
        5.   We will be prosperous: "In all that he does, he prospers" (vs. 3; cf. John 10:10)

II. **We must remember that the wicked man is cut off from the blessing of God now and forever.** (vs. 4-6)

    A.   Remember that the wicked man is like windblown chaff. (vs. 4)
    B.   Remember the wicked man's destiny. (vs. 5-6)

1 Peter 2:9-12

Theme Statement: As God's special people, you are to live holy lives.

I.   **You who believe in Christ, the Cornerstone, are a special people.** (vs. 9)

    A. You are a "chosen race." (vs. 9)
    B. You are a "royal priesthood." (vs. 9)
    C. You are a "holy nation." (vs. 9)
    D. You are a "people for his own possession." (vs. 9)

II. **Your purpose is to declare the praises of the One who called you out of darkness and into His wonderful light.** (vs. 9)

III. **You once were without an identity and without mercy, but now you are God's people, having received mercy.** (vs. 10)

IV. **Since you are no longer a part of the pagan society around you, live holy lives.** (vs. 11-12)

    A. Abstain from sin because it is destructive to your soul. (vs. 11)
    B. Live good lives so that by seeing your good deeds your lost friends may be saved. (vs. 12)

2 Timothy 4:1-8

Theme Statement: Finish the ministry to which God has called you and receive His great reward!

I.   **We have been charged in the presence of the living God to engage in Gospel ministry.** (vs. 1)

   A. We are charged in the presence of God our Father. (vs. 1)
   B. We are charged in the presence of Christ Jesus. (vs. 1)
      1. He is the judge of all men. (vs.1)
      2. He is coming to establish His kingdom. (vs. 1)

II. **God has given us a five-fold charge in our service to Him.** (vs. 2-5)

   A. Preach God's Word. (vs. 2-4)
      1. We are to preach at all times in all places. (vs. 2)
      2. We are to preach with correction and encouragement. (vs. 2)
      3. We are to preach with total patience. (vs. 2)
      4. We are to preach with instruction. (vs. 2)
      5. We are to preach without compromise. (vs. 3-4)
   B. Keep a clear mind in all situations. (vs. 5)
   C. Endure suffering. (vs. 5; see also 2 Timothy 1:8; 2:3; 3:12)
   D. Evangelize the lost. (vs. 5)
   E. Fulfill the ministry God has given you. (vs. 5; see also 1 Cor. 12:4-7, 11)

III. **We can gain hope from the testimonies of those who have finished well.** (vs. 6-7)

IV. **We will receive a great reward if we finish well.** (vs. 8; see also Matthew 16:27; Revelation 22:12)

Jeremiah 23:16-32

Theme Statement: Don't listen to the dream preachers who preach peace and safety and lead God's people further into sin.

I.   **Do not listen to the dream preachers.** (vs. 16-18)

   A.   They will fill you with false hopes because they speak visions from their own minds. (vs. 16)
   B.   They continually speak words of peace and safety even when the people of God are in sin. (vs. 17)
   C.   They have not stood in the council of the Lord to receive God's message. (vs. 18)

II. **God's wrath will come down on every false preacher.** (vs. 19-20)

   A.   His wrath will come with the violence of a storm. (vs. 19)
   B.   His anger will not turn back until He has accomplished all that is stored up in his heart. (vs. 20)
   C.   In the last days, you will clearly see it all. (vs. 20).

III. **God declares that these preachers are not from Him.** (vs. 21-22)

   A.   God has not sent them or spoken to them, but they go and preach anyway. (vs. 21)
   B.   If they had stood in God's council, they would be preaching God's Holy Word, calling all of us to repent when we are in sin. (vs. 22)

IV. **God, who sees and hears these false preachers, is against them.** (vs. 23-32)

   A.   These preachers are not out of God's sight, hearing, or reach. (vs. 23-25)
   B.   God is angrily tolerating these preachers. (vs. 26)
   C.   God knows that their aim is to cause you to forget Him. (vs. 27)
   D.   God calls His preachers to preach His Word, which is like a consuming fire and a rock-shattering hammer. (vs. 28-29)
   E.   God is against these preachers who steal their reckless lies from one another and do no good for God's people. (vs. 30-32)

APPENDIX 2

AN EXAMPLE OF THE ENTIRE PROCESS
From the Biblical Text to the Sermon Manuscript

On the following pages, you will see an example of the entire process you have studied. Our work with the text below (Philippians 4:4-9) will include:

1. **Studying the Context (<u>the same information as on p. 7-9</u>)**
2. **Write Notes on the Details of Each Verse**
3. **Side A – The Outline and Main Idea of the Biblical Passage**
4. **Side B – The Theme Statement and Outline of Your Sermon**
5. **The Sermon Manuscript**

Philippians 4:4-9

[4] Rejoice in the Lord always; again I will say, rejoice. [5] Let your reasonableness be known to everyone. The Lord is at hand; [6] do not be anxious about anything, but in everything by prayer and supplication with thanksgiving let your requests be made known to God. [7] And the peace of God, which surpasses all understanding, will guard your hearts and your minds in Christ Jesus. [8] Finally, brothers, whatever is true, whatever is honorable, whatever is just, whatever is pure, whatever is lovely, whatever is commendable, if there is any excellence, if there is anything worthy of praise, think about these things. [9] What you have learned and received and heard and seen in me—practice these things, and the God of peace will be with you.

Studying the Context
(Using the Bible as Your Only Source of Information)
Working an Example
Philippians 4:4-9

(**Note to teacher/facilitator:** Give each student a copy of the worksheet shown on p. 30, entitled "Studying the Context." While remaining together in your large group, have someone read Philippians 4:4-9. Then guide the students through the questions on the worksheet, <u>allowing them to discover and share their answers with the entire group</u>. In the notes below, the answers are provided. Do not simply give these answers. Help the students make discoveries, and have them write down the answers on their worksheets.)

1. **What kind of literature is this?** (Law, letter, parable, history, poetry, prophecy, proverbs, prayer, speech, apocalyptic writing, or some other form?)

    Philippians is a letter.

2. **What is the historical situation?**

    a) **Who is the author?**

        •   The senders are Paul and Timothy. (Phil. 1:1)
        •   The author is Paul. (Phil. 1:3 "I"; 1:4 "my"; 1:6 "I", and so on throughout the letter)
        •   Paul was a Roman citizen. (Acts 16:37-39) He was God's special messenger to the Gentiles. (Acts 9:15) (Teacher/Facilitator: There is of course much more we could learn about the Apostle Paul from other Scriptures, but we will not pursue that information in this exercise.)

    b) **Where was the author at the time of this writing?** What were his personal circumstances as he was writing/speaking?

        •   In prison (Phil. 1:7, 13)
        •   Where was the prison? In Rome (Phil. 1:13 the "imperial guard"; 4:22 "Caesar's household")

    c) **Who are the readers?**

        •   "all the saints . . . at Philippi, with the overseers and deacons" (Phil.1:1-2)
        •   There were Gentiles in the congregation. For example, Lydia and her household (Acts 16:14-15) and the jailer and his household. (Acts 16:27-34)
        •   There were Jews in the church, some of whom were trying to impose Old Testament ceremonial law on the Philippian believers. (Phil. 3:2-3)

d) Where were the readers? What were their personal circumstances at the time of the writing?

- Philippi (Phil. 1:1) – a Roman colony, a leading city in Macedonia (Acts 16:12)
- They were suffering. (Phil.1:28-30)
- As already noted above, they were under pressure from certain Jews in the congregation to observe Old Testament ceremonial laws. (Phil. 3:2-3)

e) What was the author's purpose? Was he addressing certain problems? theological problems? relational problems? circumstantial problems?

General purposes – 1) To express his thanksgiving, joy, and confidence in Christ's workings in and through them as well as his own great affection for them (Phil. 1:3-8); 2) To communicate his gratitude for their generosity toward him (4:15-17); 3) To urge them to experience joy at all times (4:4; also "joy" is mentioned throughout the letter)
Relational problems – 1) Improperly motivated preachers (1:15); 2) Lack of unity (1:27, 2:2, 4:2-3); and 3) Worry about Epaphroditus (2:25-30)
Theological problems – Legalism imposed by the Judaizers (3:1-11)

f) What do I know about the relationship between the author and the readers?

From the Letter to the Philippians

- Paul prayed for them all the time with thanksgiving in his heart and with confidence in God's work in their lives. He had deep affection for them. (1:3-8)
- Paul was hoping to send Timothy to them soon. He himself was also hoping to visit them soon. (2:23-24)
- Paul speaks of some of them as being his fellow workers in ministry. (4:2-3)
- The Philippians had sent gifts to Paul when he was in need. (4:18)

From Acts 16:11 – Acts 17:1

- Paul and Silas were the missionaries to Philippi who saw the conversion of Lydia and her household at the birth of this church. (16:11-15)
- Paul and Silas were imprisoned because of their involvement in the deliverance of a slave girl from demon possession. (16-24)
- The Philippian jailer and his household were converted. (25-34)
- Paul and Silas were released from prison after which they went to Lydia's house and encouraged all of the believers before departing for Thessalonica. (16:35 –17:1)

g) What can we discover about the social, political, economic, and cultural environment of the readers and of the author?

- The readers and the author were living under Roman rule. (Phil. 1:13; 4:22)
- It was a time of persecution. (1:7, 13, 29-30)

3.   **What comes before and after the biblical passage that I am studying?**

Immediately before? In Philippians 1:1-3, Paul is dealing with conflict between Euodia and Syntyche. Such conflict was of course preventing them from rejoicing always.

Immediately after? In Philippians 4:10-19, Paul is expressing his gratitude for the generosity of the Philippians toward him. He also says that he has learned to be content in all circumstances. He has told them in vs. 6 that they should not be anxious, and in these verses, 10-19, he is declaring his own freedom from anxiety about the provision of his daily needs.

In the book? Throughout his letter to the Philippians, many times Paul mentions "joy." He does not want anything to prevent the Philippians from experiencing joy in Christ. In each chapter it is also obvious that he has a deep longing to see them making spiritual progress. He says it very plainly in chapter one, verse 25: "I know that I will remain and continue with you all, for your progress and joy in the faith."

In the testament in which our passage is found? The joy of Christ is a major theme of the entire New Testament. In John 16:22, Jesus said to His disciples, ". . . your hearts will rejoice, and no one will take your joy from you." In verse 24 of that same chapter, He says, "Ask, and you will receive, that your joy may be full."

In the whole Bible? Joy is a theme that is seen throughout the Bible. In both the Old and New Testaments, we see that we were made to experience joy in our relationship with God. In Psalm 35:9, David says, "Then my soul will rejoice in the Lord, exulting in his salvation." In Isaiah 61:10, the prophet says, "I will greatly rejoice in the Lord, my soul shall exult in my God." In Revelation 19:7, we find that this will ever be a major theme in the hearts of God's people. The great multitude in heaven says, "Let us rejoice and exult and give him the glory, for the marriage of the Lamb has come, and his Bride has made herself ready."

Write Notes on the Details of Each Verse
Philippians 4:4-9

(Note to reader of this example: <u>The answers to question 6 below</u> for each of these verses do not reflect the full extent of my study of these verses. You will want to write lots of notes in this section. When you have finished your work, you will have many more notes than you will actually use in the writing of your sermon.)

Vs. 4

1) **Verbs** – Rejoice, say
2) **Central phrase** – "Rejoice in the Lord"
3) **Key words** – always
4) **Linking words** – none
5) **What questions are being answered by the author/speaker for his readers/listeners?**
   (How, what, why, when, where, and who?)

   • What must the Philippians do? "Rejoice"
   • When must they rejoice? "always"
   • In whom must they rejoice? "in the Lord"

6) **What questions do I have? And what questions might those in the congregation have?**
   (How, what, why, when, where, and who?)

   • Why does Paul give this command rejoice twice?

   It is probably because he said that they were to rejoice "always."

   In verses 29-30 of Chapter 1, Paul had written about his awareness of their suffering, of their struggle. And here in Chapter 4, he was telling them to rejoice "always." It may sound impossible to them. So with a heart full of love for the Philippians, Paul repeated the command: ". . . again I will say, Rejoice."

   • What does Paul mean when he says "in the Lord"?

   In verse 1, Paul wrote, "Stand firm thus in the Lord." In verse 2, he told Euodia and Synteche to be in harmony with each other "in the Lord." Here in verse 4, he told the Philippians to be rejoicing "in the Lord."

   To be "in the Lord" is to be in union with Jesus, to be in a personal, loving relationship with Him. The follower of Christ lives in a state of mental, emotional, and spiritual connection to the heart and mind of Jesus.

   • How was it possible for the Philippians to rejoice always?

   They could rejoice always because their rejoicing was to be "in the Lord." It was because their rejoicing was to be the overflow of their experience of Jesus in their hearts. Jesus promised that He would be with them "always." Therefore, they could rejoice always.

Cross-references:

> The LORD your God is in your midst,
> a mighty one who will save;
> he will rejoice over you with gladness;
> he will quiet you by his love;
> he will exult over you with loud singing. (Zephaniah 3:17)

> Though the fig tree should not blossom, nor fruit be on the vines, the produce of the olive fail and the fields yield no food, the flock be cut off from the fold and there be no herd in the stalls, yet I will rejoice in the LORD; I will take joy in the God of my salvation. (Habakkuk 3:17-18)

Vs. 5

1) **Verbs** – let, be known
2) **Central phrase** – "Let your reasonableness be known"
3) **Key words** – reasonableness (also translated gentleness or forbearance)
4) **Linking words** – none
5) **What questions are being answered by the author/speaker for his readers/listeners?** (How, what, why, when, where, and who?)

   • What must the Philippians do? "Let your reasonableness be known."
   • With whom must they be reasonable? "everyone"
   • Why must they be reasonable? "The Lord is at hand."

6) **What questions do I have? And what questions might those in the congregation have?** (How, what, why, when, where, and who?)

   • What does "the Lord is at hand" mean?

   Paul may have meant that Jesus was coming soon. Or he may have been reminding the Philippians that the Lord was right there with them.

Vs. 6

1) **Verbs** – do not be, let, be made known
2) **Central phrase** – "let your requests be made known to God"
3) **Key words** – anxious, anything, everything, prayer, supplication, thanksgiving, requests
4) **Linking words** – but, and, with
5) **What questions are being answered by the author/speaker for his readers/listeners?** (How, what, why, when, where, and who?)

   • What must the Philippians do? "Do not be anxious about anything"
   • What must they shall they do instead? "let your requests be made known to God"
   • How? "by prayer and supplication with thanksgiving"
   • What matters should this include? "everything"

6) What questions do I have? And what questions might those in the congregation have?
(How, what, why, when, where, and who?)

- What does it mean to be anxious?

- Anxiety has been defined as "a painful uneasiness of mind; a fearful concern."[29]

- Why does Paul say "prayer and supplication"? What does supplication mean?

    Supplication seems to indicate that we are coming to God with our needs and seeking His blessing.

    Cross-reference – 1 Peter 5:7, "casting all your anxieties on Him, because He cares for you."

- Why does Paul tell them to pray "with thanksgiving"?

    It seems that Paul probably was calling them to give thanks for all of God's acts of kindness to them – those in the past, the present, and the future. They should thank God for what he had done, for what He was doing, and for what He was going to do.

    <u>Thanking God for past blessing</u>: This would not only express the gratitude that is due Him, but it would also have strengthened the Philippians' faith.

    <u>Thanking God for what He was doing at that time</u>: 1 Thessalonians 5:18 says, "Give thanks in all circumstances, for this is the will of God in Christ Jesus for you." Also, in Ephesians 5:20, Paul says that we are to be "giving thanks always and for everything to God the Father in the name of our Lord Jesus Christ." As the Philippians would thank God in all circumstances, they would be glorifying God by declaring their confidence in Him. They were to thank Him not in the sense of some delight in disaster, for neither they nor God would have delight in these things. But rather, in giving thanks they would be declaring their confidence in Him. Romans 8:28 says, "And we know that for those who love God all things work together for good, for those who are called according to his purpose."

    <u>Thanking God for what He was going to do in the future</u>: By doing this, the Philippians would be stating their confidence that God was going to answer their prayers in accordance with His infinite wisdom and goodness. In verse 19 of this chapter, Paul expressed his own confidence: "And my God will supply every need of yours according to his riches in glory in Christ Jesus."

Vs. 7

1) **Verbs** – surpasses, will guard
2) **Central phrase** – "the peace of God will guard your hearts and your minds"
3) **Key words** – peace of God, in Christ Jesus
4) **Linking words** – and

---

29   Merriam-Webster Dictionary, s.v. "anxiety", online version accessed at www.merriam-webster.com.

5) What questions are being answered by the author/speaker for his readers/listeners?
(How, what, why, when, where, and who?)

- What will be given to those who pray? "the peace of God"
- How great is this peace? "surpasses all understanding"
- What will this peace of God do? "guard your hearts and your minds"
- Who is this for? Those who are "in Christ Jesus."

6) What questions do I have? And what questions might those in the congregation have?
(How, what, why, when, where, and who?)

- What is the peace of God? It is that sense of well-being, that feeling of personal security, that inner calm that comes to a believer's heart when he puts his confidence in God

- Why does Paul say "your hearts and your minds"? What is the difference between these? The heart has to do with the emotions and the will. The mind has to do with one's thoughts.

Vs. 8

1) **Verbs** – is (eight times), think
2) **Central phrase** – "think about these things"
3) **Key words** – true, honorable, just, pure, lovely, commendable, excellence, worthy of praise
4) **Linking words** – Finally
5) **What questions are being answered by the author/speaker for his readers/listeners?**
(How, what, why, when, where, and who?)

- What must the Philippians think about? Things that are true, honorable, just, pure, lovely, commendable, excellence, worthy of praise

6) What questions do I have? And what questions might those in the congregation have?
(How, what, why, when, where, and who?)

- How would the Philippians be able to "think about these things"? How would they be able to focus their minds on godly thoughts?

  Through the renewing of their mind – Romans 12:2 ". . . be transformed by the renewal of your mind."

- How does this renewing take place?

  By the Holy Spirit – Titus 3:5 speaks of the "renewal of the Holy Spirit." This renewal begins with the mind.

- What is the Spirit's principal way of renewing our minds?

  By the Word of God – In John 17:17, Jesus prayed for all of His followers (including those of us who live today): "Sanctify them in the truth; your word is truth."

Vs. 9

1) **Verbs** – learned, received, heard, seen, practice, will be
2) **Central phrase** – "practice these things"
3) **Key words** – God of peace
4) **Linking words** – and
5) **What questions are being answered by the author/speaker for his readers/listeners?**
   (How, what, why, when, where, and who?)

   • How have they gained the truth from Paul? "learned and received and heard and seen in me"
   • What will the God of peace do? "will be with you"

6) **What questions do I have? And what questions might those in the congregation have?**
   (How, what, why, when, where, and who?)

   • What does Paul mean when he uses these four verbs: learned, received, heard, and seen?

   When he says "learned and received and heard", he is speaking of the things he had taught them. Cross-reference – James 1:22, "But be doers of the Word, and not hearers only, deceiving yourselves."

   When he says "and seen in me," he is calling them to follow his example. Cross-reference – 1 Corinthians 11:1, Paul says, "Be imitators of me, as I am of Christ."

SIDE A – The Outline and Main Idea of the Biblical Passage
Philippians 4:4-9

I. **Paul commanded the Philippians to rejoice in the Lord always.** (vs. 4)

    A. The Philippians were to rejoice "always." (vs. 4)
    B. The Philippians were to rejoice "in the Lord." (vs. 4)

II. **Paul told the Philippians four things they must do in order to rejoice in the Lord always.** (vs. 5-9)

    A. They were to be reasonable with all men and women. (vs. 5)
    B. They were not to worry about anything but pray with thanksgiving about everything. (vs. 6-7)
        1. They were to pray and give thanks to God. (vs. 6)
        2. They were promised that if they would pray and give thanks, God would bless them with peace. (vs. 7)
    C. They were to think godly thoughts all the time. (vs. 8)
    D. They were to practice what they had learned through the teaching and example of Paul and other godly men who had ministered to them. (vs. 9)

Main Idea of the Passage: In order for the Philippians to rejoice in the Lord always, Paul said that they must be reasonable, prayerful, godly-minded people who practice what they had learned through the teaching and example of Paul and other godly men.

SIDE B – Theme Statement and Sermon Outline
Philippians 4:4-9

Theme Statement: In order to rejoice in the Lord always, we must be reasonable with everyone, pray about everything, think godly thoughts all the time, and practice what we have learned through the teaching and examples of godly men.

I. **You and I have been commanded to rejoice in the Lord always.** (vs. 4)

    A. We are to rejoice "always." (vs. 4)
    B. We can do this because our rejoicing is "in the Lord." (vs. 4)

II. **You and I must continually do four things in order to rejoice in the Lord always.** (vs. 5-9)

    A. We must be reasonable with all men and women. (vs.5)
    B. We must not worry but instead pray with thanksgiving about everything. (vs. 6-7)
        1. We are to pray and give thanks to God. (vs. 6)
        2. When we pray, God will bless us with peace. (vs. 7)
    C. We must think godly thoughts all the time. (vs. 8)
    D. We must practice what we have learned through the teaching and examples of godly men. (vs. 9)

SERMON MANUSCRIPT
"Rejoice in the Lord Always"
Philippians 4:4-9

(**Note to facilitators/teachers:** This sermon was the final one in a series of messages from Philippians. The word "transition" is included in parentheses, indicating that it is not actually to be said by the preacher. The words that pertain directly to application (i.e., what the listener needs to know, stop, change, and do) are in italics so that they can be easily seen. Hopefully this will help you to observe the ways in which I have sought to employ the principles given in my lecture entitled "Application of Scripture" on p. 75.)

INTRODUCTION

Throughout our study of Paul's letter to the Philippians, it has been clear that Paul has a deep longing for his brothers and sisters in Philippi to be joyful followers of Christ! Over and over again, he calls them to gladness of heart! And now as we have come to the final chapter, in verse 4, we hear him giving his final, his most direct, and his most fervent call to rejoicing!

I.   **You and I have been commanded to rejoice in the Lord always.** (vs. 4)

A.   **We are to rejoice "always."**

In verse 4, he says, "Rejoice in the Lord always; again I will say, rejoice."

Paul has given this command earlier in the letter – in chapter 2, verse 18, and again in the first verse of chapter 3. But now he gives it yet again, and he says it twice! Why does he say it twice?

It is probably because he said that they were to rejoice "always."

In verses 29-30 of chapter one, Paul had written of his awareness of their suffering, of their struggle. And now he is telling them to rejoice "always." It may not have sounded possible to them. So with a heart full of love for the Philippians, he repeats the command: ". . . again I will say, rejoice!"

(**Transition**) "But how?" they may have asked. And you may be asking the same thing here this morning, "How? How can I rejoice always? How can I rejoice in any circumstance – even the worst ones? How can I do this?"

B.   **We can do this because our rejoicing is "in the Lord."**

Paul says, "Rejoice <u>in the Lord</u>."

Paul who had suffered so greatly for the Gospel and who was in prison awaiting possible execution as he was writing this letter, understood that our rejoicing is "in the Lord."

But what does Paul mean when he says "Rejoice <u>in the Lord</u>"?

If you will please look back at verses 1 and 2 here in Chapter 4, you will see this same phrase, "in the Lord." In verse 1, Paul says, "Stand firm thus in the Lord." Then in verse 2, he urges two women to be in harmony with each other "in the Lord."

So what does this phrase mean? To be "in the Lord" is to be in union with Jesus, to be in a love relationship with Him. *By trusting in His sacrificial death for our sins, we are completely forgiven, and we are brought into a never-ending personal friendship with Christ our King as the Holy Spirit actually comes to live within us. We who are followers of Christ live in a blessed state of mental, emotional, and spiritual connection to the heart and mind of our Lord.* This is what it means to be "in the Lord."

So we can rejoice always because we are "in the Lord."

Zephaniah 3:17 says,

> The LORD your God is in your midst,
> a mighty one who will save;
> he will rejoice over you with gladness;
> he will quiet you by his love;
> he will exult over you with loud singing.

We rejoice in Him as we hear Him rejoicing over us!

Habakkuk 3:17-18 says,

> "Though the fig tree should not blossom, nor fruit be on the vines, the produce of the olive fail and the fields yield no food, the flock be cut off from the fold and there be no herd in the stalls, yet I will rejoice in the LORD; I will take joy in the God of my salvation."

This is the rejoicing to which Paul is calling you and me! Rejoicing always – in the Lord!

(Transition) But there are obstacles. There are obstacles that may prevent or hinder our rejoicing in the Lord. Paul was well aware of these obstacles. He seemed to be very concerned about certain ones. In chapter 1, Paul was concerned that the Philippians might be filled with anxiety and even fall into despair. At the beginning of chapter 2, and again here in the first three verses of chapter 4, we see the obstacle of disharmony in relationships. In the first part of chapter 3, Paul addresses the problem of doctrinal confusion brought about by false teachers who were leading some of the people into legalism. And in the final paragraph of chapter 3, Paul cautions the Philippians against following the dishonorable conduct of ungodly men.

Anxiety and despair, disharmony, doctrinal confusion, and dishonorable conduct. These are some of the things that can prevent us from rejoicing in the Lord always.

II. You and I must continually do four things in order to rejoice in the Lord always. (vs. 5-9)

Here in chapter 4, in verses 5-9, Paul tells us to be reasonable with everyone, pray and don't worry, think godly thoughts, and practice godly living. Let's look at each of these.

A. We must be reasonable with all men and women. (vs.5)

In verse 5, he says, "Let your reasonableness be known to everyone. The Lord is at hand."

In some of your translations, rather than "reasonableness" you will see the word "gentleness", or possibly "forbearance." *Paul is calling us to be kind and patient in our dealings with every person around us.*

And he gives us these words of motivation: "The Lord is at hand." Now Paul may mean that Jesus is coming soon. Or he may have been reminding the Philippians that the Lord was right there with them.

Regardless of which of these he meant, the important thing for you and me to remember is that our merciful, gentle Savior is near! And that should motivate you and me to relate to ALL men and women in the same way that He relates to us.

By being reasonable with one another, we can overcome the obstacle of disharmony in our relationships so that we can be rejoicing in the Lord. Is there someone toward whom you need to show more gentleness and patience?

(Transition) We must be reasonable and gentle with all people, and secondly,

B. We must not worry, but instead pray with thanksgiving about everything. (vs. 6-7)

In verse 6-7, Paul says, "do not be anxious about anything, but in everything by prayer and supplication with thanksgiving let your requests be made known to God. And the peace of God, which surpasses all understanding, will guard your hearts and your minds in Christ Jesus."

Worry. Do you worry very much? Many people accept worry as just a normal part of their lives. But I have heard of one man who took it a little further.[30]

This man had a friend who asked him, "Why are you always worrying about so many things? Don't you know that worrying doesn't do any good?"

And the man replied, "Oh, yes, it does. It does a lot of good. In fact, I would say that at least 95% of the things that I worry about never happen!"

Brothers and sisters, some of us are prone to worry, aren't we? Too often we live in a state of anxiety.

---

30 I think this story came from a sermon or a book by John Stott. I am not certain about its original source.

Anxiety has been defined as "a painful uneasiness of mind; a fearful concern."[31] This fearful concern can become so severe that it is overwhelming. Over a period of time, we can fall into despair; we can begin to feel hopeless.[32] And rejoicing seems impossible!

(Transition) So what are we to do?

1. **We are to pray and give thanks to God.** (vs. 6)

    First, we must pray. In verse 6, Paul says, "In everything, by prayer and supplication . . . let your requests be made known to God."

    Prayer! Supplication! Let your requests be made known! *Brothers and sisters, we are to come with all of our needs and pray to our God!*

    In 1 Peter 5:7, Peter says that you are to be "casting all your anxieties on Him, because He cares for you."

    In verse 6, we see that we must also give thanks. Paul says, "by prayer and supplication with thanksgiving."

    This thanksgiving should involve the past, the present, and the future. We thank God for what he has done, for what He is doing, and for what He is going to do.

    First, the past. As we thank Him for what He has done in the past, not only are we expressing the gratitude that is due Him, but in this recalling of the blessings of the past, our faith grows with regard to our present needs.

    Secondly, we thank Him for what He is presently doing, acknowledging that He has allowed the particular circumstances about which we are praying. 1 Thessalonians 5:18 says, "Give thanks in all circumstances, for this is the will of God in Christ Jesus for you." Also, in Ephesians 5:20, Paul says that we are to be "giving thanks always and for everything to God the Father in the name of our Lord Jesus Christ."

    We thank Him not in the sense of some delight in disaster, for neither God nor we have delight in these things. But rather, in our giving thanks, we are declaring our confidence in His promise in Romans 8:28 "And we know that for those who love God all things work together for good, for those who are called according to his purpose."

    By our thanksgiving, we are expressing our trust in God that He is bringing forth His good purposes in our present situations. In so doing, we are stating our confidence that He is going to answer our prayers in accordance with His infinite wisdom and goodness. In verse 19 of this chapter, Paul tells the Philippians of this confidence, as he says, "And my God will supply every need of yours according to his riches in glory in Christ Jesus." We give thanks as we pray because Christ is our provider.

---

31 Merriam-Webster Dictionary, s.v. "anxiety", online version accessed at www.merriam-webster.com.
32 I remember reading Chuck Swindoll's comment about this somewhere.

How much time do you and I spend each day giving thanks to God? Might I suggest that you have three thanksgiving lists? One for blessings and answered prayers of the past, another for your present blessings and for present difficulties, and a third will be your list of prayers for which you are awaiting an answer. You may not choose to write these down, but would you consider giving thanks in this way?

(Transition) Now what about the result of our praying and giving thanks? What will happen in our lives?

2. **When we pray and give thanks, God will bless us with His peace.**

Verse 7 says, "And the peace of God, which surpasses all understanding, will guard your hearts and your minds in Christ Jesus."

Peace beyond man's understanding is the product of confidence. We are confident about the future because we have placed our confidence in God. It is this confidence that causes us to be full of peace. We are secure. We are at ease.

Both our praying to God and our giving thanks to God are expressions of our faith in Him that He is going to do the right thing. Our fear is gone. What is there to be afraid of?

George Mueller was a great man of faith who lived and ministered in England in the nineteenth century. He was called by God to provide housing, food, and education for thousands of orphans without ever asking anyone for any money. Mr. Mueller said, "The beginning of anxiety is the end of faith. The beginning of true faith is the end of anxiety."

Brothers and sisters, have faith. Pray and give thanks to God, and that will be the end of anxiety!

Being delivered from worry and despair, you will be able to commune freely with your Lord. You will hear the sound of His voice rejoicing over you, and His voice will fill your heart with joy!

(Transition) We must be reasonable with everyone, pray about everything, and . . .

C. We must think godly thoughts all the time. (vs. 8)

In verse 8, Paul says, "Finally, brothers, whatever is true, whatever is honorable, whatever is just, whatever is pure, whatever is lovely, whatever is commendable, if there is any excellence, if there is anything worthy of praise, think about these things."

We must let our minds dwell on godly thoughts in order to overcome doctrinal confusion which, as we have said, was the problem Paul was addressing in chapter 3. Also, thinking about godly things will help us to overcome other obstacles to our rejoicing. If we will fill our minds with thoughts that are true, noble, pure, lovely, and admirable, we will be able to have harmony in our relationships, and we will have minds and hearts that are pure – that are clean.

But how can we do this? In Romans 12:2, Paul says, ". . . be transformed by the renewal of your mind." And how does this renewing take place?

By the Holy Spirit – Titus 3:5 speaks of the "renewal of the Holy Spirit." It has been noted by many that this renewal begins with the mind.

And what is the Spirit's principal means of renewing our minds? The Word of God. In John 17:17, Jesus prayed for all of His followers, including you and me, saying, "Sanctify them in the truth; your word is truth."

As we read, study, memorize, and meditate on God's Word, the Holy Spirit will use His Word to renew our minds.

Are we allowing our minds to be renewed? Are we dwelling on godly thoughts? What do you think about throughout the day? And what entertains you in the evenings? What television programs do you watch? What music do you listen to? What do you read? What do you talk about with your family and friends? Do you engage in godly conversation? Do you read good books? Are you thinking on things in which God has delight? Are you thinking about things that are excellent and praiseworthy?

By the workings of the Holy Spirit through God's Word, we can think godly thoughts.

(Transition) We must be reasonable with everyone, pray about everything, think godly thoughts, and . . .

D. **We must practice what we have learned through the teaching and examples of godly men.** (vs. 9)

In verse 9, we hear Paul saying, "What you have learned and received and heard and seen in me — practice these things, and the God of peace will be with you."

When he says "learned and received and heard," he is speaking of the things he had taught them.

And what about you? What teaching have you received from others? Are you practicing what you have been taught? James 1:22 says, "But be doers of the Word, and not hearers only, deceiving yourselves." Be a doer of what you have heard.

Please look again at verse 9. Paul also tells the Philippians to practice what they had "seen" in him. They were to follow his example.

Who are the godly men whose examples you will imitate? In 1 Corinthians 11:1, Paul says, "Be imitators of me, as I am of Christ." Imitate godly men!

If you will practice what you have been taught and follow the examples of godly men, you will overcome the obstacle of dishonoring behavior.

Also, in verse 9, Paul gives us this promise: "the God of peace will be with you." *You will be blessed with the presence of the God of peace. You will know that He is with you.*

CONCLUSION

Your Father in heaven has called you to a life of joy in His Son. You are to be rejoicing all the time!

And how can you experience this constant joy?! By being gentle with everyone, by praying about everything and worrying about nothing, by thinking godly thoughts all the time, and by practicing godly living.

Rejoice, my brothers and sisters! Again I say, Rejoice! Rejoice in Jesus!

ADDITIONAL LECTURES
Hermeneutics And Application

HERMENEUTICS
(Principles of Interpretation)

(**Note to teacher/facilitator:** You may wish to include some biblical examples and some of your own further explanations and quotations, but this might require that you teach these principles in more than one lecture. The following is only a concise survey.)

In the first two lectures in this book, we gave attention to the task of exegesis, and we included the following definition of that term: "Exegesis is the careful, systematic study of Scripture to discover the original, intended meaning."[33] However, we did not address hermeneutics.

Hermeneutics is a term that is derived from a Greek verb that means "to interpret." Biblical hermeneutics has been defined as "the study of those principles which pertain to the interpretation of Holy Scripture."[34]

We must have guiding principles in doing the work of exegesis. "A solid hermeneutics is the root of all good exegesis and exegesis is the foundation of all truly Biblical preaching."[35]

There is a great gap between the interpreter and the biblical writings which he seeks to interpret. This gap is historical, cultural, linguistic, geographical, and philosophical. Certain rules are necessary for the bridging of this gap.[36]

We will only look at some of the more important principles of interpretation. The ones on which we will focus can be applied to all of the Bible. There are other principles that are essential to the interpreting of specific types of biblical literature, but we will not address those here.

General Principles

- **The Bible is the inerrant, infallible Word of God.**

    A proper understanding of the Bible begins with an understanding that this collection of books is in fact the Word of God. We again refer you to the following passages:

    But know this first of all, that no prophecy of Scripture is a matter of one's own interpretation, for no prophecy was ever made by an act of human will, but men moved by the Holy Spirit spoke from God (2 Peter 1:20-21).

    All Scripture is breathed out by God and profitable for teaching, for reproof, for correction, and for training in righteousness (2 Timothy 3:16).

---

33 Gordon Fee and Douglas Stuart, *How to Read the Bible for All Its Worth*, p. 19.
34 Bernard L. Ramm, et al, *Hermeneutics*, p. 10.
35 Ibid, p.8.
36 Ibid, p. 9.

In Article VI of The Chicago Statement on Biblical Inerrancy, we read this declaration:

> We affirm that the whole of Scripture and all its parts, down to the very words of the original, were given by divine inspiration.[37]

- **The Word of God is clear and understandable.**

Those matters in Scripture that are essential to salvation can be understood by all. (The technical term here is "perspicuous".) However, as we study all of Scripture, we find that there are some passages that are not as easily understood as others. What we then discover is that what is unclear in one portion of Scripture is often made clearer by other passages.[38] So we look to the clear passages to interpret those that are unclear to us.

- **In the Bible, we are given progressive revelation.**

The idea of progressive revelation is that "God's revelation was not given all at once but over the course of many centuries as redemptive history unfolded. During that course of history, revelation progressed from the beginnings of the Old Testament to the fullness of the New Testament."[39] Progressive revelation is making reference to the fact that "the later revelation often builds upon and fills out the earlier."[40]

Article V of *The Chicago Statement on Biblical Inerrancy* states the following:

> We affirm that God's revelation within the Holy Scriptures was progressive. We deny that later revelation, which may fulfill earlier revelation, ever corrects or contradicts it. We further deny that any normative revelation has been given since the completion of the New Testament writings.[41]

In all of our thinking about progressive revelation, we must remember the two things given in this article: 1) The New Testament never corrects or contradicts the Old Testament; and 2) Written revelation from God ended with the final book of the New Testament, the Book of Revelation. The canon of Holy Scripture is closed.

- **The person and work of Jesus Christ are the central focus of the entire Bible.**

We must remember that "proper interpretation of any part of the Bible requires us to relate it to the person and work of Christ."[42] Why? Because "every part of the Bible leads us to Christ . . . ."[43]

---

37 *The Chicago Statement on Biblical Inerrancy,* Article VI.

38 Augustine says, "For almost nothing is dug out of those obscure passages which may not be found set forth in the plainest language elsewhere." See Philip Schaff, ed., *A Select Library of Nicene and Post-Nicene Fathers of the Christian Church,* Vol. II, St. Augustin's City of God and Christian Doctrine, Book 2, Chap. 6, Section 8, p. 537.

39 Sidney Greidanus, *The Modern Preacher and the Ancient Text, Interpreting and Preaching Biblical Literature,* p. 112.

40 Leon Morris, *I Believe in Revelation,* p. 139. I discovered (and subsequently obtained) Mr. Morris' work through reading in Sidney Greidanus' *The Modern Preacher and the Ancient Text, Interpreting and Preaching Biblical Literature* wherein the quote above is found on p. 113.

41 *Chicago Statement on Biblical Inerrancy,* Article V.

42 Graeme Goldsworthy, *Preaching the Whole Bible as Christian Scripture,* p. 84.

43 Ibid, p.128.

We again refer to *The Chicago Statement on Biblical Inerrancy:*

As the prophesied Messiah, Jesus Christ is the central theme of Scripture. The Old Testament looked ahead to Him; the New Testament looks back to His first coming and on to His second. . . . . Holy Scripture must be treated as what it essentially is—the witness of the Father to the Incarnate Son.[44]

- **The Bible is consistent; there are no contradictions.**

  It has been well said that if the Bible were "corrupted by the ignorance and inconsistencies of human beings," it "would no longer be the Word of God."[45]

  A great theologian of the nineteenth century wrote, "If the Scriptures be what they claim to be, the word of God, they are the work of one mind, and that mind divine. From this it follows that Scripture cannot contradict Scripture. God cannot teach in one place anything which is inconsistent with what He teaches in another."[46]

- **There are many applications of a text, but there is only one accurate interpretation.[47]**

- **A Bible passage means what its author meant when he wrote to his original readers.**

  The discovery of the meaning of a text involves "seeing each book in its own historical and cultural setting and putting ourselves in both the writer's and the readers' shoes."[48] When we study a Bible passage, we must seek to know what the Holy Spirit was saying through the biblical author to his readers at that time in order to know what the Holy Spirit is saying to us through that same passage of Scripture today. We are seeking to first find the one correct interpretation of the author's intended message, as best we can, and then make our various applications.

  There are of course some passages that have meanings beyond the understanding of the author and his readers. These passages have a "fuller sense in light of the teachings of the New Testament revelation."[49] This is certainly true of predictive prophecy related to the incarnation of Christ, to His redemptive work on the cross, to His Church, and to His second coming.

  However, we must be careful that we do not read meanings into a text (eisegesis). Any "fuller sense" of a text must be based very directly on revelation that is given at a later point in Holy Scripture.[50]

---

44 *The Chicago Statement on Biblical Inerrancy, "Exposition".* Here is the more complete quotation: "As the prophesied Messiah, Jesus Christ is the central theme of Scripture. The Old Testament looked ahead to Him; the New Testament looks back to His first coming and on to His second. Canonical Scripture is the divinely inspired and therefore normative witness to Christ. No hermeneutic, therefore, of which the historical Christ is not the focal point is acceptable. Holy Scripture must be treated as what it essentially is—the witness of the Father to the Incarnate Son."

45 Walter C. Kaiser, Jr., and Moises Silva, *An Introduction to Biblical Hermeneutics, The Search for Meaning,* p. 24.

46 Hodge, p. 187.

47 In Richard Pratt's *He Gave Us Stories,* p. 114-15, Dr. Pratt offers helpful thoughts about what he calls the "one unified meaning" of a text. When we say "one accurate interpretation", we recognize that, as he says, other biblical texts "may speak directly or indirectly" about a particular passage, providing other aspects of its full meaning.

48 J. I. Packer, *Truth and Power, The Place of Scripture in the Christian Life,* p. 140.

49 Sidney Greidanus, *The Modern Preacher and the Ancient Text, Interpreting and Preaching Biblical Literature,* p. 111.

50 Ibid, p. 112.

- **We interpret Scripture by Scripture.**

  "Sacred Scripture is its own interpreter," said the Reformers. The idea that Scripture is to interpret Scripture has been called "the analogy of faith." No part of the Bible can be interpreted in a manner that is in conflict with the faith, i.e., the teachings that we have received from the rest of the Bible. We must remember that "the meaning of any part of the Bible must be understood in the context of the Bible as a whole."[51]

- **We must identify the type of literature we are interpreting.**

  This was discussed in Lecture One. We must know the type of literature (e.g., poetry, narrative prose, history, law, letter, parable, etc.) we are studying in order to properly interpret a biblical text. The special principles that apply to the various types of literature will not be given in this lecture. They will have to be provided in future lectures. Here we will only repeat what we said in Lecture One. We cannot properly interpret a Bible passage unless we first ask, "What kind of literature is this?"[52]

- **We look to the teachings of the New Testament to help us understand the Old Testament.**

  Why does the New Testament guide us in our interpreting of the Old Testament? Because "the later revelation is fuller and clearer."[53] As we have said, revelation is progressive. Therefore, we must look at the Old Testament through the lens of the New Testament.

  However, this idea of progressive revelation does not in any way diminish the value of the Old Testament. In fact, it has been well said that "New Testament revelation can be properly understood only against the backdrop of Old Testament revelation."[54]

- **We must understand each text in its historical and literary context.** (Discussed in Lecture One)

- **We seek to understand the whole of Scripture by looking at the parts, and we seek to understand the parts of Scripture by looking at the whole.** (This has been called "The Hermeneutic Circle.")

- **We are to look to the didactic portions of Scripture to guide our interpretation of historical narratives.** (By "didactic" we mean the teaching portions of Scripture – for example, the epistles and the Sermon on the Mount.)

- **We interpret experience in the light of Scripture; we do not interpret Scripture in the light of experience.**

  We must not allow our experiences, or the experiences or alleged experiences of others, to determine our understanding of Scripture. Instead, with humility we must allow Scripture to determine our understanding of personal experiences.

---

51   Dan McCartney and Charles Clayton, *Let the Reader Understand, A Guide to Interpreting and Applying the Bible*, p. 171.
52   Several helpful sources on the interpretation of various biblical genre: Gordon Fee and Douglas Stuart, *How to Read the Bible for All Its Worth*, p. 45-245; Graeme Goldsworthy, *Preaching the Whole Bible as Christian Scripture*, p. 135-244; Dan McCartney and Charles Clayton, *Let the Reader Understand*, p. 223-242; R. C. Sproul, *Knowing Scripture*, p. 89-90, 94-99; Robert Stein, *A Basic Guide to Interpreting the Bible*, p. 73-202; William Klein, Craig Blomberg, and Robert Hubbard, Jr., *Introduction to Biblical Interpretation*, p. 323-448.
53   Dan McCartney and Charles Clayton, *Let the Reader Understand, A Guide to Interpreting and Applying the Bible*, p. 208.
54   Sidney Greidanus, *The Modern Preacher and the Ancient Text, Interpreting and Preaching Biblical Literature*, p. 113.

- **We are to look for the "plain historical sense"[55] of the language of the text.**

  This means that the "words of Scripture must be taken in the sense attached to them in the age and by the people to whom they were addressed. This only assumes that the sacred writers were honest, and meant to be understood."[56]

- **We are to understand a text to be literally true unless it is clear that we have figurative language before us.**

- **The supernatural events in Scripture are to be accepted as literally true.**

  Supernatural events are to be accepted as presented, and purely natural explanations of such events are not to be sought.[57]

- **When we encounter words that can have multiple meanings, we should determine the meaning by giving careful consideration to context.**

  Being aware of the variety of meanings that a word can have can be useful in determining its meaning in a particular verse, but "meanings other than the one specified by the text do not normally occur to the speaker and the audience."[58]

  Here we should mention that when we are preaching, in most cases, it is not important that we point out the various ways in which a word is used. We should keep our focus on the meaning of the word as it is used in the particular passage that we have before us.

- **We must be careful not to incorrectly use the study of etymology (the origin and development of words).**

  As one Bible scholar explains, "While the origins and development of a word may be interesting, writers depend on the way language is actually used in their time."[59]

  We must ask, "How would a particular author and his readers have understood that word in their cultural and historical context? And how would they have understood it in the context of the specific passage I am studying?"

- **We must pray for understanding.**

  In Psalm 119, several times we hear the psalmist praying for understanding. One of the best known of those prayers is found in verse 18 where he says, "Open my eyes that I may behold wondrous things out of your law." Like the psalmist, we must pray to our Lord and ask Him to give us understanding of His Word.

---

55   Charles Hodge, *Systematic Theology, Vol. 1*, p. 187.
56   Ibid, p. 187.
57   Ramm, et al, p. 26-27. Dr. Ramm writes, "Part of God's revelatory and redemptive work in a humanity and cosmos darkened by sin is the employment of the supernatural."
58   Kaiser, and Silva, p. 64.
59   Kaiser, and Silva, p. 64.

- **We must depend upon the Holy Spirit.**

In the New Testament, we hear the Apostle John speaking of the ministry of the Holy Spirit with regard to our interpreting of Scripture. 1 John 2:27 says "the anointing you received from him abides in you" and "his anointing teaches you about all things." Dr. J. I. Packer says that the Holy Spirit is the "anointing" about which John is speaking. He says, "Understanding comes from the Spirit through the Word; Word and Spirit belong together."[60]

But what about our own personal diligence in study? Dr. Packer gives us some very direct words of counsel:

> This learning through the Holy Spirit does not cancel the need for study, any more than it invalidates the rules of interpretation . . . . Never oppose the work of the Spirit giving understanding to your work as a student seeking it; the Spirit works through our diligence, not our laziness.[61]

- **Interpretation is to be done in the Christian community.**

We must do the work of interpretation within the fellowship of our Lord's Church. Dr. Packer says, "Understanding does not usually, and certainly not fully, occur outside the fellowship of faith,"[62] and he calls our attention to Colossians 3:16, "Let the word of Christ dwell in you richly, teaching and admonishing one another in all wisdom . . . ."

God has called us to a happy dependence upon one another in this matter of interpreting what He has said to us in Holy Scripture.

> We are to learn from one another in our local churches.
> We are to learn from those in churches of cultures other than our own.
> We are to learn from those interpreters who have lived throughout the many centuries before us.

Learning in community will help us to avoid errors and will enrich our understandings of Scripture. **(Note to teacher/facilitator:** Please see the warning against "the trap of individualism"[63] below.)

- **Study with a view to application.**

James 1:22 says, "But be doers of the word, and not hearers only, deceiving yourselves." We search for a right understanding of Scripture so that we can apply it to our own lives.

---

60 J. I Packer, Truth and Power, *The Place of Scripture in the Christian Life,* p. 133.
61 Ibid, p. 149.
62 Ibid, p. 150.
63 William W. Klein, Craig L. Blomberg, and Robert L. Hubbard Jr., *Introduction to Biblical Interpretation,* p. 141. "As Bible interpreters we must be wary of the trap of individualism. *We need to recognize our membership in the Body of Christ, the Church.* . . . We do not work in a vacuum; we are not the first ones to puzzle over the meaning of the Bible. We require the enrichment, endeavors, and assistance of our fellow believers to check our perceptions and to affirm their validity. . . . The Church throughout the ages, constituted by the Spirit, provides accountability; it offers the arena in which we can formulate our interpretation. Such accountability guards against maverick and individualistic interpretations. It provides a check against selfish and self-serving conclusions by those who lack the perspective to see beyond their own circumstances. And since the Church of Jesus Christ is a worldwide fellowship, it crosses all cultural and parochial interests – a reality we deny if we limit our interpretations and formulations of God's truth to personal (or parochial) attempts to understand Scripture. If we discover the meaning of God's revelation, it will make sense or ring true to others in Christ's worldwide Body when they openly assess the evidence we used to reach our conclusions." (Emphasis in the original)

Summary

It is essential that we make proper application of hermeneutical principles such as the ones we have just considered. By doing so, Dr. Packer says that we will experience deliverance from three tyrannies: 1) "the tyranny of being tied to our own thoughts", 2) "the tyranny of being tied to our own time", and 3) "the tyranny of being tied to our own heritage . . . (i.e., of a particular heritage of teaching and training)."[64]

May our Lord help us all to be better interpreters of His Holy Word for the sake of His people, for the sake of His glory.

---

64 J. I. Packer, p. 152-154.

APPLICATION OF SCRIPTURE

As we said in our lecture on hermeneutics, we always interpret with a view to application. In John 17:17, Jesus prayed to His Father for you and for all of His followers: "Sanctify them by the truth; your word is truth." So as you study and preach, constantly remember that God the Father is answering that prayer of His Son: He is sanctifying His people as they apply His Word to their hearts.

True preaching calls God's people to "be doers of the word, and not hearers only" (James 1:22, ESV). Through the application of God's Word, we will become holy individuals, and the Church will become a holy community.

Some Last Words to a Preacher: The Scriptures are "profitable."

It has been said that last words are often the most important words. As Paul neared the conclusion of his second and final letter to Timothy, in chapter 3, verses 16-17, he reminded the younger preacher that "all Scripture is breathed out by God" and that it is . . .

profitable for teaching, for reproof, for correction, and for training in righteousness, that the man of God may be competent, equipped for every good work.

What was Paul saying? In Scripture God tells His people what they need to . . .

*   Know – "teaching"
*   Stop – "reproof"
*   Change – "correction"
*   Do – "training in righteousness"[65]

Know, stop, change, and do: these words can be easily retained in our memory and will give us our most fundamental guidance in applying Scripture.

It is in view of this four-fold usefulness of Scripture that, in chapter 4, verse 2 of the same letter, Paul commanded Timothy to . . . [66]

correct, rebuke, and exhort, with complete patience and teaching.

So fellow preachers, we have been appointed by God to very patiently guide His people into the various ways in which Scripture is profitable to them. He has called us to help them to not only understand but also to apply His Word to their lives.

---

65   I first heard this (know, stop, change, do) from Rev. Donald Tabb in the early 1970's. I don't know the original source.
66   Some readers may know that Sinclair Ferguson makes the same connection I have made here between Paul's statement in 2 Timothy 3:16-17 and his exhortation in 2 Timothy 4:2. See *Feed My Sheep, A Passionate Plea for Preaching*, p. 198-99.

Important Things to Remember In Applying the Scriptures

Here are a few important things to keep in mind as you seek to guide your listeners in the application of God's Word (A couple of these were given in our earlier notes.):

- **Seek to have personal applications throughout your sermon.**

- **Have at least one application for every major point of your sermon.**

- **Often there will be applications for your sub-points.**

- **Close your sermon with an application of your central theme** (the idea expressed in your theme statement on Side B).

- **All applications should be very directly tied to what the author has said in the text.**

- **Applications should be very clear** (i.e., very easily understood by your listeners).

- **Applications should be specific.**

- **Use the six questions to guide your thinking about various applications:** how, what, why, when, where, and who.

- **Call for an *immediate* response.** The people must understand that, as God's servant, you are calling them to respond to God then and there in His holy presence.

- **Applications should address matters of the head, heart, and hands.** That is, you should call your listeners to contemplate, feel, and do certain things.

- **You must pray and think carefully about the emotional, social, intellectual, and spiritual needs of the people to whom you preach.** Ask God to give you an understanding of the people who sit before you. You must know the people. You must understand their needs and desires. True love for God's people will cause us to study their lives.

- **You should include applications that are helpful to *all* of the people that you are addressing:** children and adults, the rich and the poor, the highly-educated and the under-educated, new believers and mature believers as well as unbelievers.

- **There should be applications not only for the individual but also for the local church as a body of believers.**

- **Be sure to include the Gospel!** In most cases, you should give the essentials of the Gospel at some point in your sermon. Do this in a way that fits the flow of your sermon. Pray that the Lord will show you how to preach to those who are lost while you are feeding His sheep.

- **You should communicate your hopefulness of the good progress of your listeners.** Although it is essential that your preaching sometimes includes words of reproof, the people must know that you remain ever hopeful of positive change in their lives.

- **In presenting applications to the people, you must maintain a spirit of true humility.**

- **In pastoral ministry, you must be readily available to help those church members who may have questions about their specific applications of your sermon.**

- **Apply the message to yourself.** We must be like Ezra who "set his heart" to "practice" what he studied and taught. (Ezra 7:10) While preparing your sermon, you should be thinking of applications that you should make to your own life. You might consider writing these down and praying to the Lord for His help in making those personal applications.

In a prior lecture, we included an application tool by the Navigators (with slight modifications).[67] We will provide it again here.

- **Is there a <u>SIN</u> for me to avoid? or confess?**
- **Is there a <u>PROMISE</u> from God for me to claim?**
- **Is there an <u>EXAMPLE</u> for me to follow? or not to follow?**
- **Is there a <u>COMMAND</u> for me to obey?**
- **Is there <u>KNOWLEDGE</u> for me to understand and remember? (knowledge about God, the church, individual believers, unbelievers, etc.)**

(**Note to teacher/facilitator:** When teaching in English, you may choose to mention the acronym SPECK – <u>S</u>in, <u>P</u>romise, <u>E</u>xample, <u>C</u>ommand, <u>K</u>nowledge. In other languages, this acronym is of course of no value.)

The Preacher: A Traveler, Listener, and Bridge-Builder

Providing good applications for your listeners will require significant effort. You will need to be a traveler, a listener, and a bridge-builder.

In our lecture on the study of the context of a passage (p. 4), we said that we must travel back to the world of the author and the people to whom he was writing. We pull up a chair beside the author; we look around at his world; and we seek to listen to what he is saying to his readers.[68]

But there is another kind of traveling and listening that we must do. We must travel out into the world of the people to whom we will preach in order to listen to what they are thinking and feeling. We of course must use wisdom in this traveling and listening so that we do not expose ourselves to things that would cause damage to our own character. Yet we must find ways to gain an understanding of the thinking of the people whom we have been called to reach and teach.

67 *The Navigator Bible Studies Handbook*, p. 23.
68 Haddon Robinson, *Biblical Preaching*, p. 23. "An expositor pulls up his chair to where the Biblical authors sat."

So we must listen to both God's Word and to the world around us. John Stott has referred to this as "double listening."[69]

As we engage in this "double-listening," we will then be able to fulfill our calling as "bridge-builders." This is the metaphor that John Stott presents to us in his book, *Between Two Worlds* (or *I Believe in Preaching)*. He says,

> It is across this broad and deep divide of two thousand years of changing culture (more still in the case of the Old Testament) that Christian communicators have to throw bridges. Our task is to enable God's revealed truth to flow out of the Scriptures into the lives of the men and women of today.[70]

We must establish connections between the ancient text and the people to whom we minister. We must not only explain the Scriptures in ways that are understandable to them; we must also provide applications that are relevant to their lives.

However, as we seek to preach in a way that is relevant, there is a danger that we must avoid. We must not become overly focused on answering the questions that people are asking. John Stott reminds us that sometimes they are asking the wrong questions, and it is our job to guide them into asking the right ones. We must remember that the kind of bridge we build must be "determined more by the biblical revelation than by the . . . spirit of the age."[71]

We should pray for one another that God would help us to be energetic travelers, careful listeners, and wise bridge-builders.

A Few Closing Thoughts on Application

Here are a few closing thoughts concerning your providing applications of the Word of God for your listeners:

1. **Apply God's Word with a focus on Jesus.**[72]

    Our applications should "focus on the person, place, and power of Jesus Christ."[73] We must point God's people to their great Mediator, who is their prophet, priest, and king.[74]

    We of course call God's people to obedience to Jesus. But we also call them to meditate on who He is and what He has done and is doing for them. In our preaching, we are to be facilitating a direct encounter between the people and the Savior. There in His presence, by His grace, the people will hear His voice as you preach, and the Holy Spirit will move them to respond to Him.

---

69   For many years, John Stott has called Christians to this "double-listening." This idea was foundational to the "Christians in the Modern World" course at the London Institute for Contemporary Christianity in the early eighties.
70   Ibid, p. 138.
71   Ibid, p. 139.
72   J. I. Packer, Truth and Power, *The Place of Scripture in the Christian Life,* p. 166.
73   Ibid, p. 166.
74   Ibid, p. 166.

2. Take your applications to the hearts of the people.

As one well respected preacher has said, "All truly biblical preaching is preaching to the heart . . ."[75] In Scripture, the word "heart" refers to "the central core of the individual's being and personality" and is "frequently used as a synonym for the mind, the will, and the conscience, as well as (on occasion) for the affections."[76] It is "the governing center of life."[77]

We must preach to the heart, but we must do this through our listeners' minds. As we inform them of God's truth, it will transform their hearts.[78]

John Stott has urged us to see the need for a "combination of mind and heart, the rational and the emotional"[79] in our preaching. He directs us to the experience of the two disciples on the road to Emmaus whose minds had been instructed and whose hearts had been deeply touched: "Did not our hearts burn within us while he talked to us on the road, while he opened to us the Scriptures?"[80]

We are to open the Scriptures before the minds of the people so that God's message will burn in their hearts and transform their lives. In order to do this effectively, we must remember what true preaching is.

Dr. Martyn Lloyd-Jones, who ministered in London for many years, wrote,

> What is preaching? Logic on fire! Eloquent reason! . . . Preaching is theology coming through a man who is on fire.[81]

John Stott has added,

> Fire in preaching depends on fire in the preacher, and this in turn comes from the Holy Spirit. Our sermons will never catch fire unless the fire of the Holy Spirit burns in our own hearts and we are ourselves 'aglow with the Spirit'. (Romans 12:11)[82]

It is by the fire of the Holy Spirit in our hearts that we bring the application of God's Word to the hearts of God's people.

---

75 Sinclair Ferguson, "Preaching to the Heart," in *Feed My Sheep, A Passionate Plea for Preaching.* ed. Don Kistler, p. 192.
76 Ibid, p. 192.
77 Ibid, p. 192.
78 Jonathan Edwards, "A Treatise Concerning Religious Affections", Part III, Section 4, in *The Works of Jonathan Edwards*, Vol. 2, p. 281. "Gracious affections do arise from the mind's being enlightened . . . . Holy affections . . . arise from the information of the understanding, some spiritual instruction that the mind receives . . . . The child of God is graciously affected, because he sees and understands something more of divine things than he did before, more of God or Christ, and of the glorious things exhibited in the gospel; . . . either he receives some understanding of divine things that is new to him; or has his former knowledge renewed after the view was decayed . . . ." Edwards provides the following biblical references: 1 John 4:7; Phil. 1:9; Rom. 10:2; Col. 3:10; Psalm 43:3, 4; John 6:45; Luke 11:52.
79 John Stott, *Between Two Worlds*, p. 282.
80 Ibid, p. 286.
81 D. Martyn Lloyd-Jones, *Preachers and Preaching*, p. 97.
82 John Stott, p. 285.

3. **Apply God's Word with genuine love for your listeners.**

"If I speak in the tongues of men and of angels, but have not love, I am noisy gong or a clanging cymbal" (1 Corinthians 13:1).

We should be continually praying that God will increase our love for His people. You will find that it is a good habit to look out at the congregation and ask God to fill your heart with love for each one that is before you.

4. **Pray, pray, pray.**

Present your applications and the people whom you serve to God in prayer. Ask Him to help them apply His message to their lives. Pray for them before you preach and as you preach and after you have preached. Preach with expectation that God will hear your prayers and that lives will be transformed by His good hand.

We close with . . .

A DEFINITION OF PREACHING

"To expound Scripture is to open up the inspired text
with such faithfulness and sensitivity
that God's voice is heard and his people obey him."[83]

JOHN STOTT

---

83   This definition was given in an interview with Dr. Al Mohler, published in *Preaching Today* in 1987, and in an article entitled "A Definition of Biblical Preaching" an excerpt was republished April 15, 2011, which was accessed by the author of this work online at http://www.preachingtoday.com/skills/2005/august/2--stott.html

BIBLIOGRAPHY

Chapell, Bryan. *Christ-Centered Preaching.* Grand Rapids: Baker Book House, 1994.

Edwards, Jonathan. "A Treatise Concerning Religious Affections." *The Works of Jonathan Edwards.* Peabody, Massachusetts: Hendrickson Publishers, Inc., 1998. Reprinted from an 1834 edition originally published in Great Britain.

Fee, Gordon, and Stuart, Douglas. Second ed. *How to Read the Bible for All Its Worth.* Bletchley, UK: Scripture Union. 1994.

Ferguson, Sinclair. "Preaching to the Heart." *Feed My Sheep, A Passionate Plea for Preaching.* Ed. Don Kistler. Morgan, PA: Soli Deo Gloria Ministries, Inc., 2002.

Goldsworthy, Graeme. *Preaching the Whole Bible as Christian Scripture.* Leicester, UK: Inter-Varsity Press, 2000.

Greidanus, Sidney. *The Modern Preacher and the Ancient Text, Interpreting and Preaching Biblical Literature.* Grand Rapids, Michigan: William B. Eerdmans Publishing Co., 1988.

Hendricks, Howard G. and William D. *Living By the Book.* Chicago: Moody Press, 1991.

Hodge, Charles. *Systematic Theology.* Vol. 1. New York: Charles Scribner's Sons,1891.

International Council on Biblical Inerrancy. *The Chicago Statement on Biblical Inerrancy.* Chicago: International Council on Biblical Inerrancy, 1978.

Kaiser, Walter C., Jr. *Preaching and Teaching from the Old Testament.* Grand Rapids, Michigan: Baker Book House, 2003.

Kaiser, Walter C., Jr. *Toward An Exegetical Theology, Biblical Exegesis for Preaching and Teaching.* Grand Rapids, Michigan: Baker Book House, 1981.

Kaiser, Walter C., Jr. and Moises Silva. *An Introduction to Biblical Hermeneutics, The Search for Meaning.* Grand Rapids, Michigan: Zondervan Publishing House, 1994.

Klein, William W., Craig L. Blomberg, and Robert. L. Hubbard, Jr. *Introduction to Biblical Interpretation.* Revised and Updated ed. Nashville: Thomas Nelson, 2003.

Larson, Craig Brian, ed. *Preaching Today.* http://www.preachingtoday.com, 2011.

Lloyd-Jones, D. Martyn. *Preachers and Preaching.* Grand Rapids, Michigan: Zondervan Publishing House, 1971.

McCartney, Dan, and Charles Clayton. *Let the Reader Understand, A Guide to Interpreting and Applying the Bible.* Phillipsburg, New Jersey: Presbyterian and Reformed Publishing Company, 1994.

Morris, Leon. *I Believe in Revelation.* Grand Rapids, Michigan: William B. Eerdmans Publishing Company, 1976.

Packer, J. I. *Truth and Power, The Place of Scripture in the Christian Life.* Wheaton, Illinois, 1996. .

Piper, John. *The Supremacy of God in Preaching.* Grand Rapids: Baker Book House, 1990.

Pratt, Richard. *He Gave Us Stories.* Phillipsburg, New Jersey: Presbyterian and Reformed Publishing Company, 1990.

Ramm, Bernard L. et al. *Hermeneutics.* Grand Rapids, Michigan: Baker Book House, 1971.

Robinson, Haddon. *Biblical Preaching, The Development and Delivery of Expository Messages.* Grand Rapids Michigan: Baker Book House, 1980.

Schaff, Philip, ed. *A Select Library of Nicene and Post-Nicene Fathers of the Christian Church.* Vol. II, St. Augustin's City of God and Christian Doctrine. Grand Rapids: William B. Eerdmans Publishing Company, 1956.

Spurgeon, C. H. *Lectures to My Students.* London: Passmore and Alabaster, 1906.

Stott, John R. W. *Between Two Worlds, The Art of Preaching in the Twentieth Century.* Grand Rapids, Michigan: William B. Eerdmans Publishing Company, 1982.

Wiersbe, Warren and David. *The Elements of Preaching.* Wheaton, Illinois: Tyndale House Publishers, Inc., 1986.

_____ *The Navigator Bible Studies Handbook.* Colorado Springs: NavPress, 1974.

Other Works Consulted and Recommended

Alexander, Eric. *What is Biblical Preaching? Basics of the Reformed Faith Series.* Phillipsburg, New Jersey: P&R Publishing, 2008.

Doriani, Daniel M. *Getting the Message, A Plan for Interpreting and Applying the Bible.* Phillipsburg, New Jersey: Presbyterian and Reformed Publishing Company, 1996.

Doriani, Daniel M. *Putting the Truth to Work, The Theory and Practice of Biblical Application.* Phillipsburg, New Jersey: Presbyterian and Reformed Publishing Company, 2001.

Logan, Samuel T. Logan, Jr., ed. *The Preacher and Preaching.* Phillipsburg, New Jersey: Presbyterian and Reformed Publishing Company, 1986.

Sproul, R. C. *Knowing Scripture.* Downers Grove, Illinois: Intervarsity Press, 1977.

Stein, Robert H. *A Basic Guide to Interpreting the Bible, Playing By the Rules.* Grand Rapids, Michigan: Baker Book House, 1994.

NOTES

NOTES

NOTES

NOTES

NOTES

NOTES

CPSIA information can be obtained at www.ICGtesting.com
Printed in the USA
LVOW09s2035250316

480816LV00004B/7/P

9 780983 921707